~❧~ IMAG1

HISTORIC HOUSE NAMES
of
NOVA SCOTIA

JOSEPH M. A. BALLARD

NIMBUS
PUBLISHING
— NIMBUS.CA —

Nimbus Publishing Limited
3660 Strawberry Hill Street, Halifax, NS, B3K 5A9
(902) 455-4286 nimbus.ca

Printed and bound in Canada

NB1327

Design: Jenn Embree
Editor: Paula Sarson

Library and Archives Canada Cataloguing in Publication

Library and Archives Canada Cataloguing in Publication
Ballard, Joseph M. A., 1971-, author
Historic house names of Nova Scotia / Joseph M.A. Ballard.
    Includes bibliographical references and index.
    ISBN 978-1-77108-668-4 (softcover)
1. House names—Nova Scotia—History. I. Title.

GT471.B35 2018   929.9'709716   C2018-902900-5

Canada

Nimbus Publishing acknowledges the financial support for its publishing activities from the Government of Canada, the Canada Council for the Arts, and from the Province of Nova Scotia. We are pleased to work in partnership with the Province of Nova Scotia to develop and promote our creative industries for the benefit of all Nova Scotians.

For Melanie

TABLE *of* CONTENTS

PREFACE

ༀ

D o you know of any named houses in Nova Scotia? Most people
familiar with the province can likely name a few. The better-known
names are largely connected to prominent historical figures who
resided in commodious homes with sprawling grounds. Some grand
estates, like *Mount Uniacke* and *Acacia Grove*, are now provincial muse-
ums. While the wealthy and the distinguished loved to name their residences, the
naming tradition was far more plebeian and far more prevalent than most of us
realize. Consider the humble home of Matthew and Marilla Cuthbert, *Green Gables*.
Though *Anne of Green Gables* is a work of fiction set in a neighbouring province, it
accurately portrays the ubiquity of house naming at that time—a practice that
author L. M. Montgomery, a former resident of Halifax, was familiar with. One of
the challenges with researching this subject is that the house names of prominent
citizens were more widely known and more often recorded than the house names
of middle- or working-class citizens.

It would be too fanciful to claim that naming an object brings it to life, but
named houses have a certain essence and vitality about them. Named or not, places
do possess character—and putting a name to something that exhibits character makes
sense on some level. It is remarkable that a name has the power to enchant all on its
own without one having even visited the place. A euphonious appellation can delight
both tongue and ear. The way the syllables of *Scrivelsby* or *Duntulm Cottage* organize
on the tongue compare to an incantation with the power to transport one to a place
of wonder and majesty. These are the names that incite imagination and provoke
romantic associations. Suggestive names connected to cherished thoughts connote
pleasant feelings. The name *Strawberry Cottage* makes anyone who loves strawberry
harvest time and summer days before it gets too hot feel contentment. It has been
demonstrated that named houses actually realize higher prices than their unnamed

counterparts. The evidence is compounding. Named houses possess an undeniable attraction. Naming a house is a damn fine idea.

This book explores the house-naming tradition in Nova Scotia. What sorts of names did Bluenoses create? What did the names mean? What if you bought a house with a name you didn't like? What if you sold a house with a name you *did* like and wanted to take it with you? What were the cultural associations connected with the custom? Read on to find out.

MAKING SENSE *of* HOUSE NAMES

W asn't this house-naming nonsense somewhat pretentious? Well, some would have certainly viewed the practice as such, and for that reason avoided it themselves. A less-biased approach might simply recognize the tradition as a part of a society that felt compelled to name things. Certainly important things had names, and most of us feel the places in which we live are important. House naming may have even had the effect of making *people* feel more important—and that is where the veil of pretension creeps in. There is some evidence to suggest that a name could be perceived as hoity-toity,[1] but acceptance of house names was widespread. Naming could also involve intimacy, and conferring a thoughtful name on a property made it dearer to those who dwelled there as the following verses illustrate:

> *From Woodside's verdant slopes of green*
> *On Dartmouth heights displayed*
> *A broad and lovely view is seen*
> *In various hues arrayed*

By dark and shady woods relieved
The snow white cottage stands
While just below in surges heard
The broken billow lands[2]

These lines are the first two verses of the lengthy poem "Woodside," which extols the Dartmouth estate of the same name. The lines hint at the depth of feeling associated with a place so dear that it was deserving of a name. The author, a girl named Annie B. Fairbanks, lived at *Woodside*, the Dartmouth residence of her father, John E. Fairbanks. How does conferring a name deepen the intimacy, build the identity, and increase the esteem associated with a place? How does one even begin to write a poem about an object if it is unnamed?

It is important to know that house numbers have not always been with us. The absence of house numbers almost necessitated house names. Where neither name nor number existed, locals sometimes made up their own identifier, often referencing a property by the name of a former owner who had long since died or moved on.

Halifax, with a greater population density than other areas of the province, saw house numbers sooner than most. David McAlpine, publisher of the *Halifax City Directory for 1872–73* detailed his difficulty in creating a directory during a year when an improved numbering system had just been implemented. He urged businessmen to use both old and new numbers for the year and lamented the difficulties associated with houses with wrong numbers or no numbers at all.[3] The same edition contains no numbers, only street names, for Dartmouth residents.

In 1889, Truro residents engaged a Mr. W. H. Smith from New Brunswick to number the houses in their town. "His process is to attach a good substantial metal number on each door, for which he is paid by the occupant or owner of the property. He finds out by accurate counting of buildings, and measurements of vacant lots the number which properly belongs to each house, and then by mutual consent of all concerned, proceeds to put it on."[4] The description of this revolutionary process leaves one both amused by its quaint assiduity and baffled at the realization that it hadn't been undertaken at an earlier date. The same news brief alarmingly wonders if the Town Council might co-operate with Mr. Smith in having street names placed on each corner! As it turns out, it took another twenty years before all the streets of Truro were identified with signage.[5] Similarly, Digby is noted as having no house numbers in 1900.[6] These revelations show the practice of house naming was rooted in more than ostentation or affectation. Wayfinding at the time was not the habitual experience that we now take for granted, and naming of anything, whether houses or streets, would have been helpful. The reasons for house names, though, were manifold.

The house-naming tradition was connected to the formal customs of *society*. It existed alongside the formal custom of "at homes" and employment of domestic servants. "At homes" were those appointed days and hours at which ladies would receive guests: "Miss Cook, of the Normal School Faculty, will receive with Mrs. Albert Black, at 'Erwood' on the first Thursday of each month."[7] An announcement of an "at home" appeared exceedingly more elegant with a house name than without. Of course, entertaining is always easier when help can be summoned with a chime.

It seems very "old world" that domestics were so widely engaged in service here in Nova Scotia. Yet the evidence is there in newspaper wanted ads found under the dedicated heading, "Domestics," often with the associated address of some important house: *Maplewood* or perhaps *The Lodge*. The evidence of a Nova Scotia filled with domestics also survives in back staircases, service entrances, bell pulls (and buttons), and attic or cellar bedrooms. Even many modest-looking homes from the early twentieth century were equipped with such amenities. The idea that not so very long ago households could afford the expense of housemaids, cooks, or even gardeners, and conversely that average Nova Scotians would engage in such work, would seem to many the stuff of period dramas set in Britain. Yet the vocation of service was common, and it was seen as respectable work. Even as late as 1908, a Halifax wedding announcement proudly proclaimed that the groom was a gardener in the employment of B. F. Pearson, *Emscote*.[8]

The tradition of house naming in Nova Scotia appears to be closely tied to other customs associated with formal society, accepted practices, and general etiquette. The rising middle class of the Victorian and Edwardian periods weren't just building larger houses, they were also engaging in an increasing array of social pursuits and opportunities for serving the public good. Rising affluence and influence practically begs for outward expressions of respect and distinction. Naming one's house was simply one means of projecting a sense of importance and confidence that mirrored one's success in the world.

American influence cannot be overlooked. Throughout the nineteenth century, influential landscape architect Andrew Jackson Downing (1815–1852) and others chronicled and dissected the situations of American estates, both in terms of physical siting and social station. For those who thoroughly enjoyed planning and building, or just dreaming of "maybe one day," books on landscape architecture provided readers with the opportunity to immerse themselves in the most popular house style trends set by wealthy men of industry "down south." Downing's works were perhaps the most widely published, even after his short life. Estates with names were held up as examples of what wealth and correct taste might achieve if properly proportioned in the wilds of North America. This influential writer placed special emphasis on the grounds surrounding country houses and their role in accentuating and anticipating the residence, which in turn "will even serve to impress a character upon the surrounding landscape."[9] The name given to each of these estates bound the component parts, buildings and grounds, together as a single unit.

Indeed, Nova Scotia increasingly had its own examples of impressive estates modelled on the American and British tradition. *Mount Uniacke* and *Acacia Grove* closely followed the American and British concept of a country estate or "gentleman's seat," as Lord Dalhousie styled *Mount Uniacke* in 1817. Various estates on the Northwest Arm and a few other sites in Halifax and around the province were built on a scale that compared to the great American estates described by Downing.

Descriptions of the great country estates of Britain and America presented such romantic and idyllic situations that even those who did not have the means to replicate the full measure of such places created scaled-down versions, and a name was the crowning glory that, despite some perceived pretension, was a necessary consideration. The most popular, most copied names were those that were descriptive of the natural surroundings. And so *Rosebank*, *Riverside*, *Woodside*, *Hillside*, and similar names popped up around the province, conveying scenes of tranquility and romance.

METHODOLOGY

In a desire to explore the societal and familial associations and origins of Nova Scotia's named residences somewhat arbitrary decisions were made as to what exactly constitutes a named residence as well as what does not.

A true house name is essentially a well-thought-out label, approved and used by the property owner to identify, as an entity, his residence and associated grounds. The name is a reflection of the character of the place and, depending on the name chosen, often a means of linking or strengthening one's ties to that place. The name, once established, represented a sort of miniature barony, rooted in the English tradition of land ownership. It advertised a family's station in society and marked one as ambitious and cultured. It contributed to the functioning of a real or imagined upper- or middle-class aristocracy complete, in some cases, with domestic servants. It also fulfilled the very practical role of a formal address. Even after street numbers came into existence, the use of estate or house names continued to thrive.

Those named properties that operated as business concerns do not meet the criteria as defined in the preceding paragraph. These include commercial buildings, farms, hotels, and so-called houses of entertainment. Commercial buildings, generally with multiple tenants, were often named to identify where specific tenant enterprises were located. The result was names like the Chequered Building in Yarmouth and Black's Brick Block in Truro. Commercial names tended to focus on the owner's name or some aspect of the building's exterior. While these building names can be interesting, they are sufficiently independent from the tradition practiced by homeowners to be regarded as having altogether different purposes and motivations.

Former Residence of the late Rev. James Smith, D D., now Strathlorn Hotel,
Upper Stewiacke, Nova Scotia

Strathlorne in Upper Stewiacke

Other properties (farms or hotels, for example) that are named in the context of a business operation exist largely as a trade name, and other possible social associations appear largely secondary or altogether non-existent. However, things are not always so well defined. There are instances where a named residence also boasts significant farming operations but such operations appear subordinate to the estate itself. These have been included. *Acacia Grove* in Starrs Point illustrates well a significant farming concern that was overshadowed by the prominence of the estate as a whole. Likewise, there are properties that have entered into and out of the accommodation business, but the associated name either predated the operation or has endured after the venture's demise, demonstrating a distinction more associated with the estate than the business operation; *Strathlorne* in Upper Stewiacke, variously known as *Strathlorne House* and *Strathlorn Hotel*, is one such example. A common strategy in creating Victorian era hotel names was to use familiarity to attract visitors.[10] So in Yarmouth, with its proximity to New England, Americans could feel at home while staying at either *American House* or *United States Hotel*.[11]

Additionally, a property might acquire a name through the community because the community identifies the residence with an individual or a family who once lived there or events or industry associated with the place. The "old White homestead" of

South Maitland has similar "old" equivalents in every community across the province. Such names often have the power to endure through the ownership of several property owners and even beyond living neighbours' recollections of how the name originated. North End Halifax had a ropewalk, an industrial site where cotton or hemp strands were twisted into rope. A house situated on the property was unsurprisingly referred to as the Ropewalk property.

Names like the "old White homestead" or the "the Ropewalk property," if not initiated or formally sanctioned by the host residents, do not possess sufficient attributes and motivations to be regarded as formally named properties. Of course, a future resident may choose to embrace the name, even one that is foreboding, as was the case with an abandoned North River, Colchester County, home detailed later in the book.

Because a home embodies the persona of its past inhabitants, it is perfectly acceptable to retain a name that originated with earlier inhabitants. In effect, it honours their time as stewards and their impact as caretakers. It may be that a property known as *The Parsonage* has not been inhabited by a minister in over one hundred years, yet may in the present day successfully and rightfully retain that name, not only to honour an early owner, but also as a statement of pride by the current owner. Pride because parsonages are generally known to have been well-to-do residences. Pride because of the rich heritage associated with the place. Pride based even on age alone.

Although this book refers to house names, it is generally the property—the entire house and grounds—that was named. *Estate name* might be a more accurate term if it did not also carry additional inferences related to the expanse of property and social class. The grounds were inseparable from the house, two parts of a whole and bearing the same name. In many cases, the grounds, sharing in the distinguished appellation, received every bit their share of attention.

House naming has never adhered to any strict rules. While a name is often descriptive of the house itself, or of its surroundings, it can also bear some connection to the resident family, the family's heritage, or former inhabitants. Sometimes a name is simply a statement that the owner wishes to proclaim to the world.

Just as there are no hard rules as to what a house can be named, there is also no standard formula that the name must follow. Still, the history of naming reveals an extremely prevalent practice of attaching a sort of suffix to a name. The effect creates a clear distinction between house names and other objects like trees or even place names. A good example of this is the use of the suffix *cottage* in *Maple Grove Cottage*, which is clearly a residence, as opposed to Maple Grove, an ambiguous appellation, which might be a place name in the next county, or a stand of trees on a nearby hill. Another means of differentiation was achieved by simply adding the capitalized word *The* before a name. *The Maples*, for example, would have been clearly understood to be some sort of accommodation, either a residence or an inn. In the interest of individuality, a number of different suffixes (or sometimes prefixes) were regularly used.

ANALYSIS OF SUFFIXES

In deriving the meanings or associations of house names or in creating a name for one's own house, it is helpful to get to know the suffixes that have historically been used in traditional house and estate naming. Those popular suffixes that require some clarification in terms of meaning or context are identified and their definitions and associations explained.

THE CROFTS

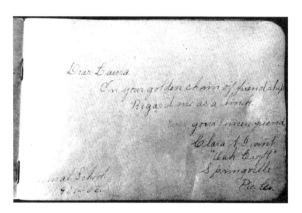

Normal School 1901–02 academic year student Clara Grant signed a fellow student's autograph book recording her address as *Oak Croft*, Springville, Pictou County.

A *croft* is an Old-English word used to describe a small piece of arable land usually fenced or enclosed in some way. Connected with such a piece of land, one would generally find a humble dwelling inhabited by a crofter (or tenant). The word is most often associated with the Scottish Highlands and Islands. The word *croft*, therefore, invokes wonderful connotations of humble dwellings, Old Scotland, and subsisting on the land, making it a very pleasing candidate for a house-naming suffix. The names *Baycroft* in Crescent Grove, Victoria County; *Oak Croft* in Springville, Pictou County; and *Acaciacroft* in Port Williams, Kings County, all produce very idyllic and romantic results that cannot be accused of stuffiness.

THE HURSTS

A *hurst* is a wooded eminence, a hillock, or grove. This suffix lends a certain air of nobility to a property. *Springhurst* in Maitland, *Lindenhurst* in Halifax, and the ubiquitous

Elmhurst, which appears in various communities, are all examples of the exalted character that can be connoted with this suffix. The *hurst* handle serves to elevate, making great properties even more distinguished.

THE COTTAGES

The meaning of *cottage* has changed considerably over the years. In Nova Scotia today, it is largely connected with small waterfront homes intermittently inhabited by summer vacationers, weekenders, and retirees—homes historically referred to as camps or retreats. The nineteenth-century use of the word *cottage* was very much linked to house construction designed to resemble traditional countryside homes in England. A sort of romanticism elevated these very modest structures to a level far beyond their humble origins, and on this side of the Atlantic inspired the design of respectable estates for wealthy Americans. During this time, the typical image that a cottage would conjure up was one of a Gothic-inspired house, the seat of a country gentleman, influenced in its surroundings by a growing appreciation for landscape gardening. American landscape architect A. J. Downing defined a cottage in terms of scale, asserting that a cottage was of a size that the household duties may all be performed by the family but in any case with assistance from not more than one or two domestics. Toward the end of the nineteenth century and the beginning of the next, the romantic connotations associated with the word *cottage* led to the term being co-opted by companies that produced popular pattern books of beautiful homes designed for suburban settings. Although this broadened the meaning of cottage (in terms of both style and setting), its image was not measurably diminished. Moreover, the middle class now found the acquisition of a residence styled as a cottage was all the more attainable.

Cottage is without question the most versatile, most popular, and most loved suffix used in naming Nova Scotia residences. That makes *Mayflower Cottage* in Musquodoboit perhaps the most Nova Scotian of all names.

THE BANKS

The *bank* suffix is topographically descriptive, generally referring to a level eminence, most often the first rise of land above a flood plain. Such landforms have been popular sites for homes since caves became passé, and so, predictably, they comprise some part of the house-naming tradition. Names that use this suffix tend to connote a definite sense of place, and that is their chief strength. In the absence of street signs and house numbers, it would, for example, be relatively easy to locate Antigonish's *River Bank*. Similarly, *Fir Banks* in Yarmouth might provide some clues as to location.

This suffix does not possess the more romantic allusions of other suffixes. In fact, it makes no pretensions on its own, thereby exuding a quiet dignity, and for some homeowners that dovetailed well with their philosophy. *Round Bank*, Upper Stewiacke, is another example that uses this descriptive suffix.

THE VILLAS

The term *villa* originated in ancient Roman times in association with homes of the upper class. In the eighteenth century, a growing regard for Italian architecture saw Italian influences imported to Britain, America, and elsewhere. At the same time, the influence of sixteenth-century Italian architect Andrea Palladio (1508–1580) was expanding throughout the western world and is still very much visible today. English country houses and Antebellum estates of the American South took up the term. Interestingly, A. J. Downing spoke of a villa in terms of scale, as being larger than a cottage and requiring the care of at least three or more servants. By the late nineteenth century, *villa* could be used to describe any free-standing house surrounded by well-proportioned and neatly landscaped grounds. A view of Dartmouth as seen from Citadel Hill in 1876 describes the thriving town: "the slopes of which are dotted with tasteful villas."[12] Nova Scotia boasts a large inventory of buildings that favour the Italianate style, and the term *villa* is well-suited to homes of this style, though by no means was it exclusive to them.

THE HOUSES

Residences like *River View House* and *White House*, located in Meaghers Grant and Tatamagouche respectively, are examples of dwellings that have embraced the *house* suffix. While it almost sounds redundant to use *house* as part of a house name, the effect of capitalizing the letter *H* in the name lends the residence no small degree of dignity; indeed, after *palace*, the suffix *house* is the most often-used suffix among the names of England's royal residences. Many early houses of entertainment or inns also adopted *house* as part of their name.

Inglewood in Wilmot, Annapolis County.

THE HOLMS

Holm (holme), pronounced the same as *home*, is defined as a low, flat tract of land beside a river or stream. *Fairholm* in Hilden and *Restholme* in Halifax are examples of this topographically specific and generally uncommon naming suffix. Alternately, *Holm Cottage* in Amherst is actually comprised of two suffixes. The house-naming tradition has a special affinity for double meanings, and the fact that *holm* is a homonym for *home* makes the use of this suffix especially attractive.

THE HALLS

A great house of an estate or a manor can also often be termed a *hall*. This suffix is generally reserved for grander properties. *Evergreen Hall* in Chester was built in 1806 and was a large and very prominent house in its day. Halifax's elegant *Keith Hall*, built in 1863, was faced with Wallace stone and was home to Alexander Keith. The *hall* suffix possesses a certain degree of respect and pretension.

THE LODGES

The use of *lodge* generally indicates an accommodation of no specific sort. It is a relatively dispassionate house-naming suffix indicative of little more than a place to lay one's head. The word is often associated with temporary stays, inns, hunting cabins, and the abodes of caretakers. Historically, it was also a common name for a meeting place for any of the many brotherhoods and societies that were so prevalent in the nineteenth century. These less than grandiose and broad connotations presumably made the term attractive to those wishing to create a house name that was either careful not to overstate a situation or perhaps intended to convey a sense of ambiguity—after all, what does a lodge look like? *Kent Lodge* in Wolfville and *Blenheim Lodge* on Halifax's Northwest Arm are two examples that were surprisingly substantial structures with the latter boasting nine bedrooms. At the more modest end of the spectrum Digby's *Morton Lodge* was a common two-and-a-half-storey house and *Lily Lodge* at Shortts Lake was a summer retreat.

SUMMING UP SUFFIXES

The meanings of other popular suffixes like *mount, grove, view, side, hill, dale, wood,* and *land* are straightforward, and beyond identification, these words should require no explanation. However, these additional suffixes suffer from an ambiguity that does not readily mark them as dwellings with the same certainty as *cottage, villa,* or any of the other suffixes described earlier. While one might not know that *Riverside* was a house at Onslow Station, it is clear that *Riverside Cottage,* at Antigonish, is.

It is important to emphasize that a suffix is not a requirement for a house name. Although, house-naming suffixes can be shown to have been used in approximately 75 percent of all house names in Nova Scotia, some of the most unique and individualized names are single-word appellations. These names, seemingly fabricated by eccentric minds with euphonious proclivities, actually represent significant personal and historical meanings to those that assigned them: *Kilmuir* and *Gladysfen* in Baddeck, *Cliefden* and *Drumbo* in Sydney, *Briarcart* and *Inselheim* in Chester. Each mysterious name elicits thoughts of aristocratic society and marvellous mansions. The task of tracing the meanings behind these and similarly obscure names presents a sort of duality in that the rarity or even the uniqueness of the name makes it either altogether impossible to track or relatively easy. Such is the delightful world of historic Nova Scotia house names. An in-depth look at how a number of estates and houses were named follows, arranged in such a way that historic names derived from similar inspirations or that share some other common attribute are grouped together into thematic chapters.

Chapter 1

NAME
CONTINUITY

⤮

I t is remarkable how the house names of Nova Scotia endure beyond the lives of those who first thoughtfully contemplated an appropriate appellation for them. In 1879, an enchanting description of Dartmouth's *Mount Amelia* was penned six years after its premier owner James W. Johnston had died. "How soon will the places that know us well and on which we lavish labour and love and money, cease to know or remember us! How soon does time the great Revolutionist plant the stranger by the hearthstone once ours!"[13]

Generally, that "stranger by the hearthstone" most often chose to retain the name bestowed by earlier owners rather than try out a new one. Research for this book has uncovered only sparse evidence of new names replacing old. Acceptance of established names by new owners seems nearly universal. Certainly, many names have been forgotten or discontinued, but this seems more the result of indifference rather than disdain. Indeed many a present-day owner, oblivious to the historic name of his demesne, appears quite delighted, even enraptured, upon learning his esteemed residence actually has a name. The effect of the revelation is pleasing to observe: all at once the perceived value of the place is elevated, its dignity revived, and the owner as expressive as if he had discovered some treasure hidden beneath the floorboards.

Although examples of swapped-out names are uncommon, some have come to light; so, too, have intriguing stories of moving names or travelling houses.

Grass-steppe, later *Bellevue*, Truro, 1903.

BELLEVUE

The aptly named *Bellevue* was one of the most attractive properties in Truro in the early twentieth century, although the residence did not always possess that name. William H. Holmes purchased the elegant mansion with the veranda on three sides from a man named H. A. Lovett in 1905. Lovett had not owned the property long. When construction began in the spring of 1901, he announced his new property would be named *Grass-steppe*.[14] The house was designed by local architect Dougald Henderson for a terraced prominence in what is otherwise a remarkably level downtown. Upon purchasing the property from Lovett, Mr. Holmes announced that it would in the future be known by the name *Bellevue*.[15] The name *Grass-steppe* was turfed, possibly making it the shortest-lived house name on record in Nova Scotia.

Holmes was a true patriot, the author of *A Short History of the Union Jack*,[16] and owner of a brass cannon that he affectionately called "Lord Nelson." Holmes routinely fired off his cannon on royal occasions. It did not seem to dissuade Mr. Holmes that at the time of renaming his residence, nearby Bible Hill already had a *Belle View*, the home of C. A. Archibald.[17]

STANYAN

Sometimes the name becomes the home. Sometimes the home develops a sort of spirit all its own. Sometimes a new house does not feel like home unless the spirit moves, too. Henry Piers lived in *Stanyan*, a house at Willow Park, Halifax, in the vicinity of the provincial exhibition grounds. The house had been in the family since 1784, and the family had been in Halifax since its founding thirty-five years earlier. In 1897, Piers purchased land at the head of the Northwest Arm. Here, alongside a stone bridge with rustic parapets, he built a new house with a commanding view of the Arm. The new house, like the old, was named *Stanyan*.[18]

In *Sketches and Traditions of the Northwest Arm* (1908), author John W. Regan explains that *Stanyan* had been an old family name in England associated with English author Temple Stanyan. Regan, however, neglects to point out that Henry Piers's grandfather, brought to Halifax in 1749 as a baby, was actually named Temple Stanyan Piers. With this additional piece of information, the connection to the author of the same name appears even more pronounced. Temple Stanyan (1675–1752) worked as an undersecretary in foreign relations and as a clerk of the Privy Council, but he is best remembered for authoring a book titled *Grecian History*. Stanyan's works recording Greek history span much of his life and are considered to be the first major English productions on the subject.[19] What influence his writings or personal life could have had on the Piers family of Halifax is a mystery; however, one rather obscure thread does exist.

Stanyan, Halifax.

Piers family members were adherents to Sandemanianism,[20] a small dissenting Christian sect that practised a primitive form of Christianity said to be based on the instructions of the apostle Paul. While working as a clerk of the Privy Council, Temple Stanyan signed many orders into law, including one on June 2, 1724, that dealt with an appeal from New England Quakers and other dissenting denominations. Their petition asked His Majesty to free four Massachusetts men jailed for refusing to assess a class of citizens generally called Quakers for taxes appearing to be for the maintenance of Presbyterian ministers.[21] Whether this or some other action endeared him to the Piers family is indeterminate, but as previously mentioned, in 1747 the name Temple Stanyan was given to a Piers baby.[22] Eventually the Stanyan name would be extended to a residence and finally the cherished name moved to a new residence.

COBBWEB

Andrew Cobb (1876–1943) was a renowned Atlantic Canadian architect based in Nova Scotia. In 1910, he built a home for his family in Bedford and named it *Cobbweb*—an obvious play on his surname—and a name he apparently was much attached to. When it came time to sell the house, he again designed a new house and contemplated what its name might be. Janet Kitz, author of *Andrew Cobb: Architect and Artist* (2014) explains,

Cobbweb, Bedford.

"In a flight of fancy, as if he were starting a dynasty, he named his homes *Cobbweb 1* and *Cobbweb 2*."[23] As it turned out, he didn't stop there; *Cobbweb 3* was eventually built. All three residences are located in Bedford. The suitability of the *Cobbweb* name is delightful in that it goes beyond Cobb's surname and connects to his occupation: a spider's cobweb is an amazing piece of architecture. Andrew Cobb similarly produced impressive projects expressive of his industry and talent.

THE CEDARS

Lumber baron Thomas Gotobed McMullen (1844–1925) was one of those rare men who seemingly possessed the bearing or means to get whatever he wanted. In 1890, McMullen wanted to build a new house at *The Cedars*[24] on Truro's fashionable Queen Street, an area of the town where other successful businessmen had built impressive residences. The trees must have been quite prominent by this time as their charms were noted thirteen years earlier: "The cedar hedge, that has weathered many a storm, stands fresh and green yet. We wish that the cedar was more generally cultivated by our gardeners. It is a pretty tree, evergreen and most odoriferous."[25] McMullen apparently admired the grounds, with its charming cedars, but this was not the house for him. He had the old residence moved to nearby Park Street and set about building himself a house worthy of his affluence. The new house, completed in 1891, assumed the mantle of *The Cedars*, while the moved house was forced to abdicate the title.

The Cedars, Truro, c. 1915.

Fernwood, later *Mount Cameron*, Antigonish.

FERNWOOD AND MOUNT CAMERON

Perched on a summit on the outskirts of Antigonish, the palatial residence of C. Ernest Gregory presented a majestic seat from which to survey one's domain. The adjoining farmland sloped away from the imposing setting of the house, and the property encompassed 280 acres in total. Mr. Gregory's residence had been built in 1879 and named *Fernwood*—ferns during this time being highly esteemed for their wispy symmetry and decorative attributes both indoors and in their natural setting.[26]

In 1907, St. Francis Xavier College obtained the property from Mr. Gregory. With the purchase, the college intended that the lands should supply it with a source of food and income; however, later that year Bishop John Cameron (1827–1910) suggested the residence would make a suitable home for aged and infirm priests.[27] Officials agreed with the bishop's idea and in their enthusiasm they proposed the estate be renamed *Mount Cameron* in his honour.[28] This new use did not interfere with the farming at *Mount Cameron,* where a Rev. Dr. Hugh MacPherson (1872–1960) directed agricultural practices as he played a leading role in the education and co-operative initiative that became known as the Antigonish Movement.[29]

WESTERWOLD

If the estate name *Westerwold* has a German sound to it, there is good reason. But that reason begins with a merchant of Scottish, not German, birth. His name was John Doull and he purchased the estate known as *Elmwood* in 1866 from Samuel Strong. Doull put his own mark on the property by adding an ell and changing its name. He selected *Westerwold*, for reasons of historic appropriateness. This area of Halifax, known as Dutch (or Deutsch) Village had earlier been known by the name of Westerwold or Westervolt,[30] meaning "West Wood." This western fringe of peninsular Halifax had been granted to "foreign Protestant" settlers of German origin who had come to the garrison town in its earliest days.

Chapter 2

LINKS *to the*
OLD COUNTRY

So many first- and even second-generation immigrants feel such a bond with the land of their ancestors that they never really let go of it. Where we come from and who we come from help form our identity. These associations with place and people can be a source of tremendous pride as well as an opportunity to accentuate or elevate social standing. Who among us does not have an ancestor who excelled in some forum: commerce, politics, religion, or the arts? And if such a connection exists, are not some of us pleased to take the opportunity to point out the esteemed relationship? A house name was a device that permitted one to draw attention to ancestors and ancestral lands.

Whether following work or following love, it is wearisome to leave friends behind in a place that has imprinted its memory on our hearts. There is an emotion—perhaps heartache, perhaps pride—which induces one to keep alive those memories that form identity, and house naming was a mechanism well-suited for wearing one's heart on their sleeve. Many of the house names in this chapter will refer to ancestral lands across the Atlantic, but the chapter closes with moves that were closer to home with the final property, *Brookfield House*, showing that even a distance of just eight miles can be enough to warrant commemoration in the form of a house name.

Bilton Cottage, Northwest Arm, Halifax, 1893.

BILTON COTTAGE

Bilton Cottage was named by owner Colonel Conrod Sawyer in fond remembrance of his home in England.[31]

EMSCOTE

Col. Gilbert W. Francklyn named his Northwest Arm home *Emscote*. In *Sketches and Traditions of the Northwest Arm* (1908), author John W. Regan states Francklyn named his residence after a village in Warwickshire, England.[32] Indeed *Emscote* was a hamlet and parish in Warwickshire; unfortunately, it is difficult to confirm Francklyn's ties to the area.

Emscote, Halifax, c. 1875.

Cote is a common house-naming suffix in England that simply means "small house" as in *dovecote*, which is a pigeon shelter. *Kingscote* in Bedford and *Elmcote* in Dartmouth are two other local examples that use the suffix but are not necessarily small in scale.

ARMADALE

Antigonish touts itself as "the highland heart of Nova Scotia," and with the number of residents who can claim MacDonald heritage, it is little wonder one of its citizens named their residence *Armadale*. *Armadale* is the former home of Antigonish's Dr.

William Henry MacDonald. It is also a castle found on Scotland's Isle of Skye, one-time seat of the powerful Clan Donald. Although the structure is partially ruined, the site remains significant to MacDonald descendants around the world.

ERIN COTTAGE

Erin is sometimes used as the poetic or romantic name for Ireland and may be said to represent the female personification of that country. Alexander and Emeline (Logan) Robb, both of Irish ancestry, lived at *Erin Cottage* in Amherst, Nova Scotia.[33] Alexander was born in 1827 at Leicester, Nova Scotia; his father had just arrived from Ireland about 1825,[34] while Emeline's family boasted a longer history in the area, dating back to Planter times.[35] *Erin Cottage*, therefore, was a proclamation of the Robb family's proud Irish heritage.

Erin Cottage, Amherst.

DUNTULM COTTAGE

Duntulm Cottage, later *Bute Arran*, Baddeck.

Duntulm (Scottish Gaelic: *Dùn Thuilm*) is a township on the most northern peninsula of the Isle of Skye. The ruins of Dunthulm Castle, dating to the fourteenth and fifteenth centuries, can be found in the area. Like much of the Gaelic language, the name possesses a certain poetic quality and in this regard is well-suited to the house-naming tradition.

Duntulm Cottage, Baddeck, was the home of Hon. Charles James Campbell MLA, MP (1819–1906). Campbell was actually born at Duntulm and left Scotland for Nova Scotia in 1830.[36] The name honours the birthplace and heritage of Campbell, the fifth son of Captain John Campbell of Duntulm.

BUTE ARRAN

Bute Arran was the Baddeck home of Hon. William F. McCurdy (1844–1923). Bute and Arran are two islands located on the western coast of Scotland in the Firth of Clyde. The islands are significant to McCurdys as the family has inhabited them since before the Norwegian invasion of AD 880. The McCurdy Clan has such a long history on these islands that strong hereditary features have long been imprinted on McCurdy descendants, so that they are in many respects alike, not just in facial features but also in terms of form and disposition.[37] So particular and identifiable are the family features that W. F. McCurdy once related his experience of walking down a New York street and of suddenly being accosted by a complete stranger who boldly asked if he was a McCurdy.[38]

DRISHANE HOUSE

A. B. Cross of *Drishane House* in Brookfield, Colchester County, formerly resided in County Cork, Ireland. That corner of Ireland is home to *Drishane Castle*, still extant near the community of Millstreet and dating to the middle of the fifteenth century. Similarly, another property named *Drishane House* of Castletownshend, also in County Cork, is a generously proportioned house dating to the eighteenth century. It is believed that Cross named his Brookfield home for his connections to that part of Ireland where the Drishane estate name enjoyed a distinguished reputation at two separate sites.

COBURG HOUSE

William Pryor built *Coburg House* about 1816–1817. It was in May 1816 that Princess Charlotte of Wales married Prince Leopold of Saxe-Coburg. The normal excitement that accompanies a royal wedding was made all the more memorable due to William's own marital circumstance. He, too, had exchanged vows with a German— Miss Barbara Foss—whose father had come to Halifax in its early days. It is said that he "paid her a compliment" by naming the property after Prince Leopold of Saxe-Coburg.[39]

BELMONT

The lands that comprise *Belmont*, the home of Henry Duncan, were obtained by Duncan in 1790. Before being appointed to council by Governor John Parr, Duncan held a number of positions in the Royal Navy, including Commissioner of the Halifax Dock Yard. Thus the Commissioner's lands were informally known as *Commissioner's Farm* before Duncan conceived of something more distinguished. The name *Belmont* "was conferred on the property probably to continue the name of Duncan's ancestral home in Dundee."[40]

STRUAN HOUSE

The Struan (also Strowan) name is closely associated with the Robertson and Duncan clans. Alexander Robertson of Struan, Perthshire, was a colonel in the 82nd Regiment,

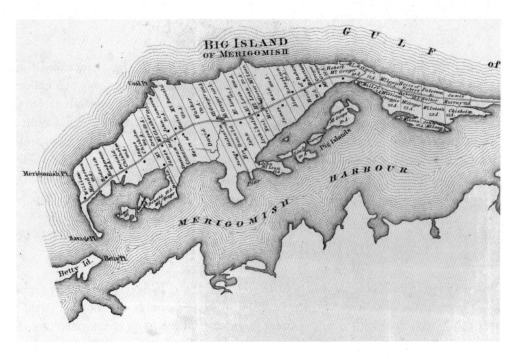

An 1879 illustration of Big Island, Pictou County, where Alexander Robertson had *Struan House* built.

mustered for service in North America during the American Revolution. At the close of the conflict, the colonel, as with others in his regiment, was induced to settle in Pictou County by receiving a land grant. His generous remuneration consisted of Big Island in Merigomish Harbour. Though he never occupied it, Robertson did have a large house constructed, which he named *Struan House*. The area was settled by his relatives. Upon his death, his possessions passed to a nephew.[41]

Evidently a good name for a Robertson residence, the Struan designation could also be found at Port Clyde where *Struan* was the summer home of William Robertson of Halifax.[42]

ARDNAMARA

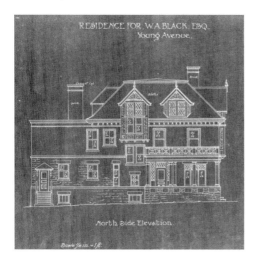

Architectural drawings of *Ardnamara*, showing north elevation.

She answered me in Garlic, so I was told afterwards, for I never heard it afore. It warn't French, or Portuguese, or Spanish, I knew, for I had heard them folks talk; but it was Garlic. Well, the girls all stopt, took a look at me, and then they began to jabber away in Garlic too.

—Thomas C. Haliburton, *Sam Slick's Wise Saws and Modern Instances*

Ardnamara, the home of W. A. Black, was situated on Halifax's grand boulevard, Young Avenue. The rear of the house faced Halifax Harbour, and it was that backdrop that inspired the Gaelic name *Ard na mara*, meaning "above the sea."

MONYMUSK

This is a very old name of Gaelic origin, pronounced *Munny-musk*, and said to mean "hill between the waters." The name is referred to as far back as the twelfth century in connection with a Culdee monastery and its lands located in Aberdeenshire, Scotland. For much of its existence, the place carried on as an Augustinian priory but was destroyed by fire in the sixteenth century. It was at this time that Duncan Forbes bought the church lands and the Forbes' association with the property began. The Forbes are said to have built the *House of Monymusk* from the blackened remains of the priory. The four-storey stone structure is built in an ell configuration with towers that are reminiscent of the defensive tower houses built for protection from neighbouring clans.[43]

In 1624, the baronetage of Nova Scotia was devised as a means of supporting the colonization of the Province of Nova Scotia. Those honoured as baronets were required to contribute money to the scheme. In 1626, Charles I named Sir William Forbes, 1st Baronet of the Baronetcy of Pitsligo and Monymusk.[44] In 1713, Sir William Forbes, 4th Baronet, sold the estate of *Monymusk*. The Forbes association with the Monymusk name endured through the baronetcy; and so, with both the honour of the baronetcy and the history of the great tower house, the peculiar name continued to inspire. *Monymusk*, North Sydney, was one expression of that inspiration. In 1901, owner G. F. Muir Forbes hosted a family reunion at *Monymusk*, where generations of the Forbes clan celebrated the eighty-sixth birthday of Mrs. John Forbes.[45]

TWEED-DALE HALL

Robert Grieves Noble (1792–1872) was born in Peeblesshire, Scotland, and immigrated to Nova Scotia sometime before 1821, when records show he married a Lucy Butler, his first wife, in Halifax. In establishing himself in his adopted land, he entered into mercantile pursuits, which eventually included his sons.[46] After the death of Lucy, he resided with his second wife, Mary Iles, at *Tweed-dale Hall* in Halifax.[47] The name of the Noble residence appears to honour Robert's family heritage–firmly rooted in Tweeddale, Scotland, a district with boundaries that correspond to the historic county of Peeblesshire where he grew up. The area takes its name from the River Tweed and the fact that it encompasses the river's source and much of its course as it flows eastward.

Robert's maternal grandfather, David Grieve, took a prominent part in the agricultural improvements of his time in Tweeddale.[48] David lived at Jedderfield Farm, where he was a tenant farmer on the lands of the Earl of March. It was said that while the proprietor of the farm was pursuing a career of sport and debauchery in London, the tenant, David Grieve, reared on that small bit of his lordship's domains fourteen children, many of whom went on to such superior positions that the family became a virtuous example to all who observed their frugal, rural life.[49] It was on the Jedderfield Farm that David Grieve famously provisioned the Jacobite army in 1745.[50]

Selecting the name *Tweed-dale Hall* must have been a deeply personal means of honouring family roots for a man who, before the age of two, had lost his father—a father, who in departing prematurely, left scant provision for his children.[51] At the same time, the situation afforded the siblings of his mother's first marriage was so disparate that the whole affair reads like a Jane Austen novel.

BEINN BHREAGH HALL

This thirty-seven-room house perched above the cliff known as Red Head is an architectural and cultural treasure. Its castle-like form presides over the small town of Baddeck and the Bras d'Or Lakes, with a commanding panoramic view of all four Cape Breton counties.

Beinn Bhreagh Hall, Baddeck.

The laird of *Beinn Bhreagh*, Alexander Graham Bell, needs no biography retold here. Bell had seen much of the world before declaring that he had found the most beautiful place on earth. His "beautiful mountain" just needed a beautiful language; and so, the Gaelic translation *Beinn Bhreagh* proved harmonious and neatly acknowledged the heritage of the inventor's birth and much of Cape Breton as well.

Like a nickname used among family members, *Beinn Bhreagh Hall* is informally called *The Point* when referred to by descendants of Alexander and Mabel. Even many of the rooms of the house have their own names.[52]

DUNVEGAN

Dunvegan Castle, Isle of Skye, Scotland, is the seat of the chief of Clan MacLeod. This great beacon of MacLeod clansfolk inspired John McLeod to name his house in Annapolis Royal, *Dunvegan*. Its central location, opposite Fort Anne, was better suited to enterprise than residence. And so throughout its existence, the property underwent a number of alterations and additions until in its final iteration as the Queen Hotel, it was destroyed by fire in 1921.[53]

ATHOL COTTAGE

Queen Victoria's visit to Scotland in 1842 was a memorable occasion that evinced an extraordinary expression of mutual admiration and pride between the monarch and her Scots subjects.[54] The visit precipitated a new esteem for Scotland and all things Scottish, as Victoria herself set the example by purchasing Balmoral Castle in 1848. During that earlier visit, Victoria had spent three weeks in residence at *Blair Castle*—the ancestral home of Clan Murray in Blair Atholl, Scotland. During her stay, the personal bodyguards of George Murray, 6th Duke of Atholl, provided a guard for the queen. So impressed was Victoria with these soldiers, the Atholl Highlanders, that she soon after presented them with their own colours. Today, they remain the only private army in Europe. This successful visit and its positive consequences imparted much esteem to Clan Murray and the area known as Blair Atholl.

Several Nova Scotia residences reflect the pleasant associations connoted by the various spellings of Athole, Atholl, or Athol, and some have clear connections to Clan Murray. Rev. Dr. Isaac Murray lived at *Athole Cottage* in New Glasgow.[55] Peter Murray of Truro lived at *Athol Cottage*.[56] Dartmouth also had an *Athol Cottage*,[57] and Bayfield had a *Camp Athol*.[58]

Athol Cottage, Dartmouth.

CASTLEBANK

At our old historic places
Tis worth your while to stop;
There's "Castlebank" and "Woodcliffe"
And The Old Curiosity Shop

—Truro Daily News, January 10, 1919

Correspondence from Britain addressed to *Castlebank*, Truro (Bible Hill).

Castlebank was a stately name for a stately house. This was the Bible Hill home of John Patton Davidson and his wife Kate (Yuill). The house is believed to have been built in the 1860s. John died a young man in 1874, and his wife survived him for many years, residing at *Castlebank* with her sisters, Frances and Clara, until 1919.[59] John's grandmother is said to have immigrated to Nova Scotia with her five sons in 1810 from *Castlebank*, Dumfriesshire, Scotland. Relatives on both sides of the ocean kept in touch, even as late as 1911, when Kate received a letter from her departed husband's extended family, thanking her for sending a photo of her standing on the veranda of *Castlebank*. The letter remarked that the roof of *Castlebank* in Bible Hill bore a strong resemblance to "the old country *Castlebank*" and wondered if it was modelled after it.[60]

DERRY PLACE

Derry Place was the Colchester County home of Dr. J. L. Peppard.[61] It was located in Great Village in the township of Londonderry. Our counties are no longer divided into townships, but these old divisions are clearly defined on old provincial maps. Derry, meaning "oak grove," is the historic name for Londonderry, Ireland, which traces its

Derry Place, Great Village.

habitation back to the sixth century and has had its "London" prefix for only the last four hundred years or so, having received it in 1613.

ELLAND HALL

Joseph Kaye left Elland, a Yorkshire town just south of Halifax, England, and immigrated to Nova Scotia where he settled in the Richmond area of Halifax, Nova Scotia. Kaye, a merchant, resided at a place called *Elland Hall*[62]—a name that disclosed and celebrated his connection with his Yorkshire roots.

Looking south on Campbell Road (now Barrington Street) at Young Street intersection, Halifax, *Elland Hall*, right, just outside of the frame.

JUBILEE

This day in future times shall stand renown'd,
The fiftieth year since GEORGE our King was crown'd;
Britain! Thy freedom may he long maintain,
And Chertsey sing his bless'd and happy reign.

—Author unknown, 1809

Jubilee, the Northwest Arm home of John Pryor, is said to have been built in the fiftieth year of the reign of George III and named for the king's golden jubilee.[63] Celebrations for the king's anniversary began with the close of his forty-ninth year on October 25, 1809. An account of the period indicates an almost spontaneous effusion of joy and

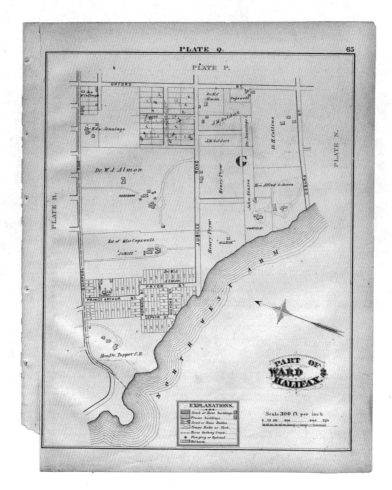

Jubilee identified left of centre on this 1878 map of Halifax.

admiration, which was neither commanded nor invited; indeed it was even discouraged in some places, but the sentiment of the people could not be restrained. The jubilee was hailed by Britons of all ranks and classes. In ports such as Halifax, the Lords of the Admiralty had ordered that all the brave tars should be regaled with roast beef, plum pudding, and a pint of wine, or half a pint of rum to mark the occasion.[64] *Jubilee* is also found to have been called *Jubilee Cottage*,[65] perhaps to differentiate it from the road that took its name from the estate.

Farraline, Bedford.

FARRALINE

The Bedford home of Sir Charles Frederick Fraser (1850–1925), named *Farraline*,[66] reveals a connection with the Frasers of Farraline—a branch of Clan Fraser that possesses its own armorial bearings. Farraline is also a place name in Inverness-shire, Scotland, located east of Loch Ness. Frederick Fraser was an indefatigable advocate for the blind and was knighted for his work in 1915.[67]

DUNROBIN

Dunrobin Castle, the largest castle in Scotland's Northern Highlands, is an imposing piece of architecture. Perched on a bluff and constructed of freestone, the castle is the very image of storybooks and fairy tales. Located in the county of Sutherland, it is also the hereditary seat of the Earl of Sutherland and Clan Sutherland. Slightly more plebeian Sutherlands in Kentville, Nova Scotia, lived in a modest home they called

Dunrobin, Four Mile Brook, Pictou County, c. 1950.

Dunrobin.[68] This allusion to the great seat of the Sutherlands effectively proclaimed clan pride and conveyed a sense of respect. Another *Dunrobin* could be found at Four Mile Brook, Pictou County.[69]

MARGAREE COTTAGE

Even a move across the Strait of Canso from Cape Breton Island to mainland Nova Scotia can tug at heartstrings just as much as a move across "the pond." The Ross family of Salmon River, Colchester County, lived in a house they called *Margaree Cottage*. It was here that they received many dear friends from Sydney[70] to St. Peter's,[71] but their hearts were in Cape Breton and specifically, northeast Margaree, their former home.[72] Rosses have dwelled in the Margaree Valley since the late eighteenth century.

Brookfield House, Truro, with stables-and-carriage house, right.

BROOKFIELD HOUSE

Brookfield House[73] was not in Brookfield, the former Colchester County home of its owner and one-time Member of Parliament Seymour E. Gourley (1854–1906). The residence was close though, just eight miles down the road in Truro, where Mr. Gourley practiced law.[74] Representation was both a habit and a vocation for Seymour Gourley. Just as he represented clients in legal matters and constituents in political matters, he represented Brookfield, the place of his birth, wherever he went.

Chapter 3

FAMILIAL CONNECTIONS

Surnames have been artfully inserted into the formal appellations of many properties. Some surnames simply lend themselves well to this sort of word-smith wisdom. The great benefit of this particular property-naming strategy is that an association or similarity between surname and residence serves to help others more easily identify or retain the names of both dweller and dwelling. Some estate names are merely mundane extensions of the family name, other creations reflect amusing wordplay or double meanings, and still others are quite clever—perhaps even requiring some word sleuthing on the part of the first-time hearer. Names that require this extra bit of thought provide a subtle but pleasing reward when the connection between resident and residence is finally made.

Faulkner House, located on Young Street in Truro, is as straightforward an estate name as can be found. It simply reflects the inhabitants' family name.

The residence of Truro mayor George Stuart was dubbed *Stuart House*. The seemingly straightforward name gains regal distinction when one recognizes its tongue-in-cheek allusion to the House of Stuart, that Scottish dynasty that ruled parts of the British Isles from the fourteenth to the seventeenth century.

Hibbert's Green in Economy is said to have been built by a man named Silas Hibbert Crane, and named in 1823, the year of his marriage.[75] Even the unusual suffix *Green* appears to be chosen for its phonetic similarity to the man's surname, *Crane*.

Lantzlot, Oakland, Lunenburg County, appears to be a name cleverly crafted as a homophone for Lancelot, the most famous of the Knights of the Round Table. The residence is an obvious play on owner Arthur Lantz's surname. He also notably shares a name with the legendary King Arthur of Camelot.

Aston Villa is a name that any fan of today's English football would recognize. The English football club is actually quite old, founded in 1874, and was arguably the most successful club of the late nineteenth century. Although there is no way of definitively knowing the extent of his sporting interests, it was during the same period that W. A. Aston of Truro decided to name his residence *The Villa*.[76]

Urbania countenanced the urbane concept of house naming when the Roses, a once prolific family of this Hants County community, decided upon a name. Perhaps not surprising, the family co-opted the already immensely popular house name *Rosebank*. It is unknown whether roses grew on the grounds, but it is difficult to imagine that they did not.

Some people possess one of those names that just begs to have fun with it. One such person was M. G. DeWolfe, who owned a summer home at Weymouth Point, on the mouth of the beautiful Sissiboo River, Nova Scotia. DeWolfe's house was cleverly called *Wolfe's Den*,[77] or variously *Wolf Den*.

Clearly, women historically played a role in naming their family's home: the home may be said to be a man's castle, but it was so often a woman's domain. Her influence in running the affairs of the home extended to naming, as so many house names attest. The maternal side of the family proved a rich resource for honouring the heritage of that party, who through marriage surrendered her surname and all of its sundry social and sentimental associations. Naming a house was one means of asserting powerful connections to the wife's side of the family or even those of the husband's mother, or affectionate connections to the wife herself.

ATHELSTON HALL

This aristocratic-sounding name is well-suited to the imposing edifice to which it is attached in Maitland, Nova Scotia. *Athelston Hall* was home to William D. Lawrence (1817–1886), shipbuilder, shipping magnate, and politician.[78] Athelston is actually an uncommon surname with which the Lawrence family is associated. The surname is believed to date back to the tenth century when King Athelstan became the first king of Britain.[79] William D. Lawrence's grandmother was known as Lady Athelston, and that connection is believed to be the inspiration for the name.

Athelston Hall, later *Lawrence House Museum*, Maitland.

LYNNHURST

Lynnhurst in Truro has a distinguished connection to Lynn, Massachusetts. Henrietta Agnes lived at *Lynnhurst* with her husband, James E. Bigelow. Henrietta was the daughter of the much-esteemed George Hood, who served in both the Massachusetts House of Representatives and the state Senate. Hood was also the first mayor of Lynn, Massachusetts. The name *Lynnhurst* proudly celebrates Mrs. Bigelow's Massachusetts heritage and the contributions her family made to that state.

SCRIVELSBY

When first the new-crown'd King in splendor reigns,
A golden cup the royal Champion gains
With gesture fierce, his gauntlet stern he throws,
And dares to martial fight his absent foes.

—Rev. Samuel Lodge, *Scrivelsby, The Home of the Champions*, 1893

Scrivelsby, Truro, 1900.

Scrivelsby is an odd but distinguished-sounding name. Even hearing it for the first time engenders aristocratic associations, and well it should. *Scrivelsby* is "the home of the champions"; at least, the historic manor of Scrivelsby in Linclonshire, England, is. The English estate is connected to the Marmion and Dymoke families. There exists with *Scrivelsby* a sort of hereditary office known as the Championship. The title of champion is bestowed upon the owner of *Scrivelsby* and apart from the owner, no one is entitled to be called champion to the reigning king or queen.[80]

The royal champion historically played a ceremonial role in the coronation of a new sovereign. The champion, an armoured knight mounted on a white horse, would charge into the coronation banquet and, interrupting the sumptuous feast, would throw down his gauntlet and challenge anyone who would deny their sovereign's rightful title to the imperial crown. The gauntlet was to be thrown down three times before the king or queen toasted the champion, whereby the sovereign's gold cup would be passed to the champion to drink off the remainder.[81]

As noted above, one of the families associated with the manor and its title is Dymoke. The Dymokes have been champions since the thirteenth century. The first Dymoke, or Dimock as it is spelled on this side of the Atlantic, arrived in Nova Scotia in 1759, fleeing from religious persecution in New England.[82]

Alice Sophia H. Dimock (c. 1848–1941) became Mrs. O. C. Cummings in 1873 when she married Oliver C. Cummings.[83] The Cummings family resided in Truro and named their impressive Second Empire–style home *Scrivelsby Manor*, which was more generally known as the shortened *Scrivelsby*.

MOUNT AMELIA

James William Johnston (1792–1873), lawyer, judge, and politician, was a prominent member of Halifax society and became Nova Scotia's third premier in 1857.[84] In the late 1830s, he began building his estate, *Mount Amelia*, in Dartmouth.[85] The place was named to honour the memory of his beloved wife, Amelia Elizabeth Almon, who had passed away in 1837. In 1845, Johnston remarried.[86] One can only assume that his new wife, Louisa Pryor Wentworth, was amenable to retention of the name *Mount Amelia* as it respectfully continued on for the duration of their residence and beyond.[87]

Amelia E. Johnston was not the only Amelia associated with the beautiful property though. The next owner, Thomas L. DeWolfe,[88] inhabited *Mount Amelia* along with his wife, Amelia Allison.

Mount Amelia, Dartmouth.

ELLENVALE

Some simple blossom, native and unsung,
Of Nova Scotia's fragrant lineage sprung,
Such as the woodman's hand may not deflow'r,
Nor Micmac banish from his rustic bow'r

—Albyn, *The Water Lily*, 1852

Andrew Shiels (1793–1879) was a blacksmith by trade, but the Scotsman fancied himself a sort of Robert Burns. Shiels submitted Burns-style verses to the *Novascotian*, published under the pseudonym "Albyn." His penchant for the poetical may have prompted him to name his property near Preston. Paying a compliment to his wife, Ellen, he named the place *Ellenvale*. Upon himself he bestowed the title "the Bard of *Ellenvale*."[89]

ELLENHURST

Locate the flower garden where the wife can see it when about her daily work,
and it will prove a means of grace to her.

—*Colchester Sun*, November 11, 1885

William Thomas James (1845–1913), native of New Brunswick and former mayor of Hamilton, Bermuda, had a summer home in Paradise, Nova Scotia. He named

Ellenhurst, Paradise, on the Annapolis River.

the place *Ellenhurst* in honour of his wife, Ellen B. Fowler. William died at *Ellenhurst* in 1913, and Ellen continued to visit the home after his death.[90] Their home in Paget, Bermuda, was named *Bellevue*.[91]

CLERMONT

Back to the hills of home I come,
Back to the hills of home;
Child to the land of heart's desire,
Child to the elm and white church spire.

—*Truro Daily News*, September 26, 1914

Charles Inglis (1734–1816) was born in Ireland, the third son of a minister. As a Church of England clergyman himself, he was ministering in New York at the time of the American Revolution. His second wife, Margaret Crooke, had been born in New York's Hudson Valley. The banks of the Hudson River were fine sites for impressive country estates. One of these was *Clermont*, derived from French words meaning "clear mountain" and built within view of the Catskill Mountains. *Clermont* was perched on the opposite side of the river from Ulster County, where Margaret was born.

Sketch of *Clermont*, Aylesford.

In 1787, Charles was appointed the first bishop of Nova Scotia, but he would take up this post without Margaret; tragedy had struck several years earlier with her death.[92] In 1796, Bishop Inglis retreated from his administrative life in Halifax to live as a gentleman farmer in Aylesford, where he is said to have named his estate *Clermont*, in recognition of the estate of the same name on the Hudson River.[93] It is probable, though uncertain, that the name bore some special significance to the bishop's time in New York or the childhood of his wife Margaret. *Clermont*, notwithstanding any association with the Catskills, is quite suitable for an Annapolis Valley site under the influence of the North and South Mountains.

CRANECROFT

Rev. Byron Crane Borden, DD, (1850–1929) had a summer home in Avonport, Hants County, named *Cranecroft*.[94] Reverend Borden was a prominent educator associated with the Methodist university of Mount Allison in Sackville, New Brunswick. After entering the college as a student, Borden later took on roles of professor, principal, dean, and finally president, with the latter capacity lasting from 1911 to 1923.

Cranecroft, Avonport.

The Crane name was of some consequence. Apart from being his middle name, Crane was also the maiden name of Borden's mother, Miriam Susanna Crane. The Cranes were New England Planters who figured prominently in settling the Annapolis Valley and in forwarding Methodism in Nova Scotia. Borden's uncle, Robert Elijah Crane (1817–1872) was the first convert of Lower Horton in 1838,[95] and entered the ministry, serving until his death in 1872. Robert Hibbert Crane (1793–1839), Borden's great-uncle, was the first native-born youth in the Maritimes to enter ministry under Methodism.[96] The Allison family of Mount Allison University, where Borden toiled for more than forty years, has close historical associations with the Crane family in ventures both of business and of marriage.[97]

Borden's retirement days were spent in Annapolis Royal, where he resided at *The Willows*.[98]

LUCYFIELD

George Lawson (1827–1895), a Scotland-born botanist and educator, immigrated to British North America to satisfy his passion for botany through the possibilities of discovering and documenting plant life in the New World. After a brief stint with Queen's College in Kingston, Upper Canada, he arrived in Nova Scotia in 1863, with his wife Lucy and their two daughters. In Halifax, he took a position at Dalhousie College, teaching chemistry and mineralogy. Eventually, George established a summer home and model farm in Sackville that he named *Lucyfield* after his wife Lucy.[99] Though her husband was better known, Lucy also was an accomplished botanist, and her interest in nature extended also to entomology.[100] Lucy died in 1871, and George remarried in 1876. It seems the name continued on, as various scientific journals continued to reference plant life at *Lucyfield* for many years after her death.[101] The name *Lucyfield* exemplifies George's devotion both to his first wife and to the study of nature; the fact that she shared his passion for nature adds another layer of significance to a fitting name.

COLMONELL

Andrew W. Robb (1876–1951) brought his young family to the Halifax area from Cape Breton to take a position with the *Halifax Herald*. His wife, Helen Dennis, was a daughter of William Dennis, president of the newspaper. With a newspaper career secured, Andrew purchased a house in Bedford and moved his family there in 1914. The move

Colmonell, Bedford.

also included Andrew's mother and Robb matriarch, Marion MacCrindle.[102] The large Bedford home was named *Colmonell* in honour of Marion MacCrindle's birthplace in Scotland.[103] She died five years after the move.

MOUNT MARTHA

She will tap at the cottage window,
One tap with her fingers cold,
And the fire will be bright
On the hearth to-night,
As it was in the nights of old

—*Morning Chronicle*, November 19, 1873

Mount Martha, comprising about one thousand acres near Grand Lake, was one of several estates owned by Thomas N. Jeffery (1782–1847), including *Waterloo*, *Lakelands*, and *Dalhousie Farm*.[104] The well-connected Jeffery was named Collector of Customs at Halifax while still a minor.[105] In 1805, he married Martha Maria, daughter of

Richard John Uniacke of *Mount Uniacke*. Martha's mother, also named Martha Maria, is remembered by Lake Martha, adjoining the Uniacke estate. It is likely that Thomas Jeffery named *Mount Martha* after his wife, although it is possible she may have reserved that honour for her mother, who died in 1803.

ORME COTTAGE

Frederick S. Payne is listed in *McAlpine's Halifax City Directory* in 1878.[106] By 1889, the annual directory identifies his home as *Orme Cottage*.[107] His mother and father appear to have moved in with their son at *Orme Cottage* late in their married life. The unusual house name originates with Frederick's maternal ancestors. His mother was born in England, c. 1812, as Eliza Wilson Orme and died at *Orme Cottage* in Halifax in 1892.[108] Family records indicate a considerable regard for the Orme name as it appears with unusual regularity as a middle name in successive generations and branches springing from Eliza's marriage to Thomas Payne.

Orme Cottage, Compton Avenue, Halifax.

Ravenscraig, Truro.

RAVENSCRAIG

*Dr. W. S. Muir is building a handsome barn on his property on Arlington Place.
It has not the staid old appearance of an orthodox barn, with the usual severely
plain barn architecture, but is broken up with towers and turrets, and points and
peaks that make it look good enough for a church.*

—*Truro Daily News*, May 19, 1897

Welcome to *Ravenscraig*, the stately residence of Dr. William and Catherine Muir.[109]
The house once stood on the eastern corner of Arlington and Prince Streets in Truro.
The entrance to Arlington was bookended by the impressive homes of two doctors
Muir, William and his brother David; the latter resided at *Deeplawn*. Their mother,
Esther, was a Crowe, and it is believed that William named his residence *Ravenscraig*
for her maiden name.

Crows and ravens are considered among the most intelligent of birds, and as a
source for house names, they appear much admired and adaptable. Truro had a cluster
of homes in the spirit of *Ravenscraig*, namely *Ravensworth*, *Crowe's Nest*, and *The Rookery*.

Chapter 4

NATURE'S
NOBILITY
BORROWED

Trees are a rich resource of positive associations and connotations: nobility, strength, longevity, and perseverance are just a few qualities that a proud family would want to take umbrage under. What better way to facilitate the use of these positive attributes as descriptors of your family situation than to have others formally adopt them in their everyday speech whenever chance happened to require making reference to you or your residence? There really is none. This is why trees were so often tapped for inspiration in determining a suitable name for a family's residence.

Fairly commonplace were the simple arbor-inspired estate names like *The Birches, The Lindens, The Lilacs, The Willows, The Cedars, The Firs, The Elms,* and on they went, covering every locally grown monarch whose beauty or nobility could be lent to a residence and its surrounding grounds. As stately as *The Elms* may sound, more pretentious cousins were created with variations such as *Elmwood, The Elmsdale, Elmhurst, Elmscraggy,* and *Elmcroft.* The elm was by far the most widely used tree in naming Nova Scotia properties, not just in terms of frequency of use but also in the sheer variety of names that inventive homeowners composed. In addition to those already mentioned were *Elm Cottage*, *Moss Elm*, *Elm View*, *All Elms*, *Elm House*, *Elm Bank*, *Elmcote*, *Elmslea Cottage*, and the definitive *Twin Elms*.

The latter is particularly interesting and unusual on account of its quantifiable precision. The tandem elms must have exhibited a rare degree of prominence, and presumably a remarkable similarity in height and canopy to be honoured in such a way. *Twin Elms* was located on Church Street, a short connector street in Truro, which was apparently so well endowed with elms that it was at the same time also home to the property known as *High Elms*. In light of the definitive nature of the name *Twin Elms*, it is somewhat perplexing to consider what might happen if just a single tree were to succumb to disease or wind, leaving its bereaved twin and homeowner to calculate the loss.

Of course, whatever the celebrated tree species, it had to have a physical connection to the property. A home with a carriageway lined with willows could not reasonably be named *Oaklands*. Still, a lengthy description of Halifax's *Rosebank* written in 1908 makes no mention of roses but describes the grounds as "studded with enormous old willows."[110] Perhaps the author's omission merely suggests the flowers were not in bloom or that he did not want to risk boring the reader by enumerating the obvious.

Sometimes where no single species displayed dominance, a more vague reference to trees was made. *Greenvale* in Dartmouth, *Greenwood* in Falmouth, and *Forest Lawn* in Truro are all wonderful examples of this. Indeed, the stalwart associations that are conjured up by estate names using individual species somehow give way to images of the picturesque when more generalized arboreal names are adopted. Places like *The Bower* in Halifax and *The Grove* in Chester connote a real sense of romance that places with individual tree names don't seem to match.

Apart from Chester, already mentioned, Baddeck and Dartmouth were also home to places called *The Grove*. In Dartmouth, *The Grove* was for sale in 1904. From the real estate listing, some insight may be gleaned as to what the fourteen-acre estate looked like. An excerpt reveals, "The house and out-buildings, which require repainting, stand in a grove of well-matured trees."[111]

Creating names that combined a tree with a prominent landform offered still more variety in the ubiquitous use of trees in naming residences. *Oakmount* in Bedford, *Chestnut Hill* in Antigonish, and *Willow Bank* in Truro all follow this formula and in doing so capitalize on the prominence associated with both trees and acclivities.

SPRUCE COTTAGE

Even the lowly spruce—often rebuffed for its offensive odour—has been acknowledged in the naming tradition. Residences named *Spruce Cottage* existed in both Truro[112] and

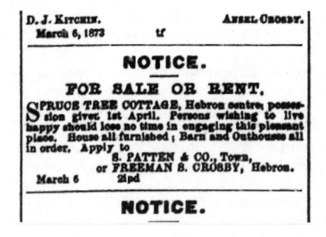

Spruce Tree Cottage for sale, *Yarmouth Herald*, March 6, 1873.

Antigonish,[113] even though one might not typically associate the evergreen with urban or semi-urban settings. Rural settings seem more conducive to the contentious conifer. *Spruce Grove Cottage* was located in Princeport,[114] while at the opposite end of Colchester County, *Spruce Hedge Cottage* in Waughs River[115] was a conveniently named home for a man by the name of Wellwood.

In 1892, a Colchester newspaper remarked that the cultivation of spruce hedges had not been put into general practice locally, as it had in other provincial towns. In what was perhaps a rare display of approbation for the tree as an ornamental, the writer noted that spruce hedges could have a "decidedly pleasing effect," and furthermore that they "afford the eye relief from the many leafless branches in winter."[116] Of course, where animals are present, a spruce hedge also makes an effective fence.

In Hebron, Yarmouth County, the singular *Spruce Tree Cottage*[117] is a name that suggests there was perhaps only one spruce associated with the property, which highlights the inherent risk in pinning too much distinction on something so susceptible to the whims of wind and worm.

FIR BANKS AND THE FIRS

"So far, good," said Anne, nodding cautious approval. "But Gilbert, people cannot live by furniture alone. You haven't yet mentioned one very important thing. Are there trees about this house?"

— L. M. Montgomery, *Anne's House of Dreams*

In 1870, the *Yarmouth Herald* awakened its readers to the salubrious news that, "the pleasant odor emitted by fir-trees in a sunny atmosphere has long been thought serviceable to invalids, and the vicinity of pine woods has been deemed healthy."[118] *Fir Banks*

Fir Banks, Yarmouth.

in Yarmouth is believed to have been built in 1869, a year before the local newspaper heaped so much esteem upon fir trees. It is not known when exactly owner Robert Caie named his place, but it is clear that his appraisal of firs was much in conformity with the editor of the weekly news. North Sydney also celebrated the fragrant fir, as witnessed by the name of the Vooght residence known simply as *The Firs*.[119]

THE LINDENS

In 1894, *The Lindens* in Londonderry, Nova Scotia, was described as one of the oldest residences in that community. George Romans resided there; his old house was situated on a magnificently landscaped property. The "smooth shaven" lawns, the tennis grounds, the maples, and the chestnuts all attracted attention in their own way. The rose bushes abounded in such profusion that scarcely any place else could compare.[120]

A sketch of *The Lindens*, Londonderry, c. 1908.

Yet above all this variegated landscape, it was the "mammoth lindens" that were looked to, to bear the namesake for the place.

The Lindens example is interesting as it clearly shows that the inspiration for a property's name need not originate from some idea that a particular species must wield exclusivity over the place—prominence, yes, but not a monopoly.

WISTERIA

For every flower has its voiceless lore,
And a lesson it teaches well,
And all we need is an earnest heart,
And to hear and heed the spell.

—*Yarmouth Herald*, June 1, 1846

In the late nineteenth century, Chester was discovered by Americans seeking respite from mosquitoes and sweltering summer heat. The town earned a reputation as a summer resort. One of the first properties to be snatched up by summer residents was *The Blockhouse*, a property formerly used by the militia. The new owner decided on a more euphonious name, *Wisteria*. The name will undoubtedly cause one to anticipate a pre-eminent connection with the flower of the same name, though *Wisteria* is actually a clever derivation of Wister, a family name belonging to the new owner, one John Wister, an iron mogul from the Germantown section of Philadelphia. The flowering plant, wisteria, does have a sort of tangential connection though. The wisteria plant

Wisteria, Chester.

was named by botanist Thomas Nuttall (1786–1859), who said he named it in memory of Dr. Caspar Wistar of Philadelphia.[121] Wistar is a variant spelling of Wister, a prominent German family that established themselves early in Philadelphia's history.

FOREST LAWN

Plants, then have their problems and their struggles as we do; and meet them much in the same way. The ambitious ones who take advantage of every opportunity succeed. Others only partially succeed, and the least persistent ones are entirely forced out of business.

—L. A. DeWolfe, *Nature Study Hints*

Following a woeful spring frost, a news brief detailed the resulting damage in the local newspaper: "Some 25 helthy [*sic*] cosmos plants were destroyed by the hartless [*sic*] antics of Jack Frost on the night of the 20th inst, in the Forest Lawn Gardens; and we know the Laird of 'Windiholme' will regret to read this."[122]

The *Forest Lawn* property referred to is actually the newspaper editor's own residence, the grounds of W. D. Dimock. He often shared the experiences of his own property in the *Truro Daily News*. It is clear that Dimock did create a forest of sorts with the profusion of flowers and vegetables that he cultivated. "A bit of a test was made this season in the corn patch at the 'Forest Lawn' gardens," he explains, when he tells

Forest Lawn, Truro, circled, on an 1878 map of the town.

his readers about planting four varieties of corn.[123] A very different kind of forest was created when Mr. Dimock planted two rows of sunflowers, four feet apart with fifty plants in each row. The exultant editor scoffed at the *Pictou Advocate*'s assertion that Pictou produced larger sunflowers than Truro as he countered with his calculation of *Forest Lawn* sunflower stalks reaching from twelve to fourteen feet in height.[124] Apart from the usual garden variety vegetables, the adventurous Dimock also dabbled in tobacco[125] and chufas.[126]

In returning to the notice of Jack Frost destroying the cosmos plants at *Forest Lawn*, it was stated that the Laird of *Windyholme* would regret the news. Who was this authoritative man with a fondness for flowers? He was Loran A. DeWolfe, a well-known educator and early advocate of rural science. In his book *Nature Study Hints*, published in 1919, DeWolfe laments that, "There is a 'sameness' about most country gardens that approaches monotony." He then goes on to identify two dozen flowers "well worth growing" including the cosmos.[127] Though DeWolfe was residing at *Windyholme* in Bible Hill during that regrettable flower-destroying frost of 1907, eleven years later this flower fancier's house name is actually known as *Flowerland*.[128]

BIRCHAM AND BLOOMINGDALE

On the waters of the Arm,
Dwelt Waegwoltic, fair to see,
Maiden of most winsome charm,
Nature's masterpiece was she

—D. M. Matheson, "Chebucto," *in Chebucto and Other Poems,* 1916

The *Bircham* property was home to Robert Morrow, a man who possessed an extreme fondness for natural history. His basement was a laboratory for the study of fish. Here, with his aquarium to aid his studies, he penned several papers dealing with marine biology. It was, however, the more visible natural history outside his house, rather than that which swam in his basement, that carried the banner of his manor. The property was called *Bircham* for the great quantity of imported Scottish silver birch planted on the grounds.[129]

Nearby, was the property known as *Bloomingdale*, named by one-time owner, Hon. A. G. Jones.[130] The euphonious name is said to be suggestive of the home's setting, as it peeps through the umbrageous trees at the shimmering waters of the Northwest Arm.[131]

Early in the twentieth century the twelve-acre *Bircham* estate and five-acre *Bloomingdale* property were united to form one large summer resort for bathing and boating on the Arm. The hotel took the first syllable of *Bircham* and the last of *Bloomingdale* and marketed the remarkable conglomerate as *Birchdale*.[132]

THORNVALE

By winding vale of hawthorn hill,
O wilderness, I love thee still!
The rosy flush, the dusky hue
Of blending morn and twilight dew.

—William M. Leggett, "The Pilgrim Bard," in *Yarmouth Herald,* April 26, 1834

Archbishop Thomas L. Connolly named *Thornvale* for a thorn hedge that bordered the property where it met the waters of the Northwest Arm.[133]

Thornvale, Halifax, c. 1872.

CLOVERDALE COTTAGE
AND CLOVERNOOK VILLA

I'll seek a four-leaved Shamrock,
In all the fairy dells;
And if I find the charmed leaf,
Oh, how I'll weave my spells!

—Samuel Lover, *Digby Weekly Courier*, March 25, 1894

Greenwood Cottage features a quatrefoil (four-leaf clover) motif in a round gable window on all four elevations of the house. *Cloverdale Cottage*, located in Bridgetown on nine acres of land, combined the privileges and pleasures of both town and country. As if to confirm the authenticity of its namesake, a 1905 real estate advertisement stated the property cuts hay for cow and horse.[134] Clover was remarkably valuable in its double

Gable detail of *Greenwood Cottage*, Sherbrooke.

role of a nutritious fodder for livestock and an effective agent in enriching the soil in which it is grown.[135] *Clovernook Villa* in Five Mile River, Hants County, also esteemed the value of this staple crop.

FERNWOOD, FERNDALE, AND MORE

Ferns once held a singular place in the aspirations of girls and women. The voracity exhibited by female collectors and decorators cannot be overstated. Called the "rapacious feminine spoiler" by one local newspaper,[136] those that plucked the much-esteemed fern went about their deed as though hunting for truffles. A decorating authority of the time explains how the ferns were used: "They are alike good for baskets, vases, rock-work, ornamental plants, for parlor or conservatory, and the pressed leaves of some of the varieties are marvels of graceful beauty."[137]

Flower arrangements described by late Victorian decorating books commonly prescribed the fern as a staple of the art.[138] With unique varieties of fern found in different regions of the province, amateur botanists would see how many they could collect.[139] So it is little wonder that the fern found a place of honour in house names.

Fernwood, Bridgewater, 1918.

Fernwood appeared in Antigonish,[140] Bridgewater, and Halifax;[141] *Ferndale* in Five Mile River[142] and Halifax;[143] *Fernleigh* in Bedford;[144] *Fern Cottage* in Dartmouth;[145] *Glen Fern Cottage* in Wilmot;[146] and *Fern Hill* in Truro.[147]

ROSE COTTAGE, ROSEBANK, AND THE ROSARY

Scatter the germs of the beautiful!
By the wayside let them fall.
That the rose may spring by the cottage gate,
And the vine on the garden wall.

—J. E. A. Smith, "Scatter the Germs of the Beautiful," *Yarmouth Herald*, August 5, 1859

Several variations on the rose theme dotted the province with the most common being *Rose Cottage*, *Rosebank*, and *Rosebank Cottage*. These three together appear twenty-six times across the province from Baddeck (with two occurrences) to LaHave. The popularity of the rose name is greatest among all documented names in Nova Scotia, narrowly edging out *Hillside* and *Hillside Cottage*. The origins of the name should be self-evident: people love roses. The number of cultivars, varieties, and species are said to be in the thousands. The plant is valued both as an ornamental and as a hedge. The rose has long been a favourite of formal gardens and flower shows.

Still, a house name is a name for all seasons, so why choose a name associated with something as fleeting as a blooming rose? Well, Nova Scotians have long had access to a wide variety of roses and as early as 1873 could actually buy ever-blooming roses from local nurseries. Homeowners were encouraged to keep their potted roses inside until June, put them in the flower garden (still in the pot) where they were expected to bloom until October, remove them to the house where they would bloom until December, and then give them a rest in the cellar until March, when the cycle could start all over again.[148]

Roses are reported to have bloomed as late as November at a Truro property known as *The Rosary*: "The second day of November we'd been handed from 'The Rosary,' grounds, Prince Street, a most beautiful specimen of the 'Edith Cavell' red rose, grown outside, as shapely and as fragrant as a midsummer production; more 'peerless' indeed!"[149]

The popularity of the name *Rose Cottage* was also aided by Robert B. Brough's novel *Miss Brown: A Romance*, which was serialized in copies of the Halifax newspaper the *British Colonist* in 1859–1860. The fictional setting of *Rose Cottage* played a central role in the tale.

ACACIA GROVE

Curious, that while our snorting, groping, grasping, conceited, jack-ass like managers of Royal woods never have been able to perceive that it was their duty to pay attention to what I said about locust trees…the Americans themselves should have their attention stirred up by my exertions in England.

—Author unknown, *The Life of William Cobbet, Late MP for Oldham*, 1835

With an international reputation for apple cultivation and ornamental grounds featuring over fifty varieties of roses,[150] horticulturist Charles Ramage Prescott (1772–1859) had obvious choices in selecting an ambassador from the plant kingdom to carry the title of his estate. But what did he choose? Surprisingly, he chose *Robinia pseudoacacia*, a "false" acacia, also known as black locust. Prescott presumably held it in some regard as *Acacia Grove* became the name of a hundred-acre estate, with a perfectly proportioned Georgian house and

Acacia Grove, later *Prescott House Museum*, at Starrs Point.

an abundance of apple trees. There are a number of varieties of acacia or locust that produce wood of an indifferent character, but the black locust, native to specific parts of the Appalachians and Ozarks, boasts a wood both remarkably strong and rot-resistant.

Although we know that Charles Prescott's house at Starrs Point was finished in the year 1818,[151] we do not know when he planted the acacia grove or when he named his estate after it. We do, however, know about the notoriety of acacia trees at that time—something that Prescott, with his interest in horticulture and international memberships in various horticultural societies,[152] must have also been privy to and may have aroused in him a special affinity for the tree.

Following the War of 1812, the British credited the Americans' use of black locust trunnels (or treenails) in American naval ships as the reason why that country's ships held together so well under canon fire. Indeed it was asserted that "without the Locust it is impossible to match them."[153] Following the war, American capitalists did big business in exporting treenails to Britain to outfit ships there, both naval and merchant, in like manner.[154]

As the world was awakening to the attributes of this special tree, William Cobbett (1763–1835) published *The Woodlands* in 1825. Sixty-five years later, this detailed treatise on the cultivation of forest trees was still being hailed as the best English language book on the subject.[155] It may have been guilty though, of going over the top with its extensive tribute to the black locust: "The time will come (and it will not be very distant) when the Locust-tree will be more common in England than the Oak; when a man would be thought mad if he used anything but Locust in the making of sills, posts, gates, joists, feet for rick-stands, stocks and axeltrees for wheels, hop-poles, pales, or for anything where there is liability to rot. This time will not be distant, seeing that the Locust grows so fast."[156]

Cobbett's enthusiasm for the tree and his zeal in promoting it caused it to be widely planted throughout England and America.[157] He personally sold over one million of the plants and countless seeds.[158] He lauded the black locust as the strongest of all North America's trees, fast-growing, and indestructible by earth, water, or air.[159] It made exceptional firewood with the fuel value of one cord equalling that of a ton of anthracite coal.[160] A high resistance to rot made it ideal for fences or any application where close proximity to the ground was necessitated. Testimonials of black locust fence posts lasting over one hundred years, coupled with Cobbett's charts that detailed impressive growth rates, got the attention of estate owners who recognized the value of the timber for estate purposes.[161]

Although no evidence of how Charles Prescott used his grove of black locusts was uncovered in researching this estate, the tree's many uses include such relevant applications as fencing, firewood, vineyard stakes,[162] tool handles,[163] and ladder rungs[164]—all applications well-suited to the management of *Acacia Grove*.

As it turns out, the black locust appears to be a marvellous tree entirely worthy of an estate name, but its alias, acacia, which is more euphonious, gets all the glory in Starrs Point.

LOCUST KNOLL

Locust Knoll suffered no crisis of identity with its acacia counterpart. "A model of taste, neatness, and completeness"[165] described Dr. A. C. Cogswell's property in 1879. The knoll offered a fine view of Halifax—a long line of houses intermingled with steeples—and the citadel commanding all, overlooking the placid harbour.

THE WILLOWS AND WILLOW COTTAGE

It is asserted that when the Acadian people left France, one or more brought willow twigs or walking sticks fashioned from the tree.[166] The original tree in France was a staminate tree, and a twig from such a tree will grow if stuck in moist soil. Most of the large spreading willows that we see around the province are said to have come from "French Willows." It was, at one time, quite common to see these arboreal monarchs lining town streets as evidenced by old photos and street names, but their removal was necessitated by their aggressive root systems that played havoc with sidewalks, streets, and sewers. Their prominence, once far beyond what it is now, generated many house names. Four Halifax properties named *The Willows* appear to have existed

The Willows, Gilberts Cove.

simultaneously. The same name also appears in Ecum Secum, East Wallace, Forest Glen, Lower Economy, Marie Joseph, Onslow Station, Springville, Gilberts Cove, Truro, Upper Stewiacke, and Waughs River.

GARDEN KNOLL

Since I left the dear old homestead,
Since I left the trees and flowers,
Skies so bright have strangely darkened,
Wild rank weeds grow o'er the bowers.

—B. B. McCormick, *Truro Daily News*, August 17, 1910

It was said that Miss Susan Murphy's natural fondness for flowers and garden produce had been intensified by her associations with the neighbouring republic. She had resided in the United States for a number of years, but during the First World

Garden Knoll, Clam Harbour.

War she found herself back home in Clam Harbour. Here, in the wilds of the forest, she developed "a gem of a little garden percht [*sic*] on a bit of a hill." Here was the home residence, encircled by a plot of wheat promising good returns, fine potatoes, twenty to thirty trees with fast-ripening fruit, and myriad flowers with the whole ensemble bounded by dense forest. Travellers staying at the nearby hostelry, known as Stoddart's, who came for trouting on Marys River or bathing on the long sand beach, would also occasionally visit Miss Murphy's beauty spot, *Garden Knoll*.[167]

Portrait of Susan Murphy, owner of *Garden Knoll*.

Chapter 5

NAMES *from* LITERATURE

For much of the nineteenth century, books were the dominant and ubiquitous vehicle of both learning and entertainment. Polite conversation of the day might have included queries as to what one had recently read and what one thought of the motives of this or that character. Quotes or subtle references from popular literature might have been casually inserted into regular conversation just as naturally as today's pop culture seeps into everything. Newspapers listed arrivals of new books, announced the latest offering of a prominent author, and advertised specially bound volumes of old favourites. Books were indicative of higher education; one's knowledge of novels and of their larger-than-life characters cultivated droll and witty conversation.

When considering the information that a named residence can convey—and in particular what such names might say about the inhabitants—those dwellings that take their inspiration from literature can make powerful statements about the quality of people that live inside. This brand of house name may reveal more about the owner's tastes than any other kind of house name. It may hint at some degree of aestheticism or cultivation or a certain way of life.

Perhaps most telling of all is not what is revealed about the homeowner, but what is revealed about a visitor who does not understand the literary reference. Consider for a moment a dapper young visitor who raps on a door and is met with the greeting,

"Welcome to *Bleak House*." If the dumbfounded visitor wonders at the reason for such a depressing name, he's obviously not familiar with Dickens—and what kind of person is not familiar with Dickens? If a healthy appreciation for English literature is lacking, what other refinements might be wanting?

Of course, the most influential book of all is the Bible, and so it is not at all surprising to find names derived from favourite passages or from Christianity in general. A house name that is recognized as a Biblical reference confers upon the inhabitants a certain expectation of integrity and charity. It is an assertion that the inhabitants are Christians and that they strive to live up to Christian ideals.

The fictional worlds of Jane Austen, L. M. Montgomery, and many other authors were so rife with imaginative settings of named estates that their works not only encouraged the real-life adoption of fictional names but also encouraged the practice of house naming in general. Non-fiction works by landscape gardeners such as Humphry Repton, John Claudius Loudon, and Andrew J. Downing promoted ideals of country and suburban living that typically included the names of estates they'd visited or designed.

Was *Camp Crusoe* in Chester a reference to Daniel Defoe's *Robinson Crusoe*?[168] Was *The Golden Fleece* in Halifax inspired by Jason and the Argonauts?[169] Did *The Jungle*, Murrays Siding, have anything to do with Rudyard Kipling's *The Jungle Book*?[170] These names and others hint at curious or probable connections, but this chapter will confine its analysis to more conclusive examples. In observing this particular motivation in house naming, there is no better place to begin than with a man who is widely believed to have been the greatest novelist of the Victorian era, Charles Dickens.

BLEAK HOUSE

"Jarndyce of Bleak House, my lord," said Mr. Kenge.
"A dreary name," said the Lord Chancellor.
"But not a dreary place at present, my lord," said Mr. Kenge.

—Charles Dickens, *Bleak House*

In 1853, Dickens published his hefty manuscript *Bleak House* that told the story of young Esther Summerson, governess of two Jarndyce cousins, heirs to a well-known fortune indefinitely tied up in legal limbo in London's High Court of Chancery. The novel's title has a dual meaning, serving as both an allusion to the dismal legal deadlock of Chancery, set within a gloomy London backdrop, and as the curious name of the Jarndyce estate, a place that at one time deserved its melancholy namesake, but

Willow Street, Truro, N.S.

Bleak House, Willow Street, Truro, c. 1905.

subsequently radiated with the unbounded generosity of its new master, Mr. John Jarndyce.

Bleak House as a name in this part of the world may reveal an advanced appreciation for literature among its inhabitants, but it also conveys a certain welcome humility, as any guest's experience with such a residence is likely to be far more rewarding than the unassuming name suggests. Still another reason for such an appellation may result from an extensive restoration of a run-down property. The *Bleak House* of Dickens's creation was revealed to originally have been called *The Peaks* but was renamed *Bleak House* by a depressed man so completely consumed by legal entanglements that he was slowly driven to his grave while his neglected house fell into disrepair around him. Enter the man's affable nephew, John Jarndyce, who took over as "rain fell through the broken roof, (and) the weeds choked the passage to the rotting door."[171] Dickens's likeable character returned the place to its former prominence but retained the dreary name almost as if to underscore how far it had once deteriorated by losing sight of what is important in life.

Bleak House is a seemingly odd name for the residence of any genial family that might wish to project a sense of warmth and hospitality; yet, it is a fine name for consumers of English literature and in particular for fans of Charles Dickens. As a

Halifax-based newspaper proclaimed in 1854, "It is enough for a large number of readers to know that a work is by this author to ensure its popularity."[172]

Charles Dickens actually visited Halifax in 1842. An account of his visit can be read in his book *American Notes* (1842). Ads for Dickens's novel *Bleak House* can be seen in the provincial newspaper ads of a Halifax bookstore early in 1854.[173]

Truro had two properties named *Bleak House*: one on Queen Street and the other on Willow Street. The Willow Street *Bleak House* sounded anything but bleak in 1916 when the local newspaper rejoiced in receiving "a big bunch of red and pink roses of rare beauty kindly sent by Mrs. John W. Purdy from the lovely gardens at 'Bleak House,' Willow Street."[174]

GREEN GABLES

We had quite a time deciding on a name. We tried out several but they didn't seem to belong. But when we thought of Ingleside we knew it was the right one.

—L. M. Montgomery, *Anne of Ingleside*

Fans of the fictional character Anne Shirley know quite well where *Green Gables* is located; however, Cavendish, Prince Edward Island, has no monopoly on this name. For in another place, one that especially embraced the tradition of naming houses, there was another *Green Gables*. Some time between the first printing of *Anne of Green Gables* in 1908 and 1910, a bank manager arrived in Truro to take the reins of the Canadian Bank of Commerce branch in that town.[175] Within the next couple of years he settled into a new house he had built on Willow Street and called it *Green Gables*.[176]

Curiously, the man's name was Charles W. Montgomery. A search for a familial connection between he and Anne creator, Lucy Maud Montgomery, has proved none existed, at least within several previous generations of Montgomerys. It appears as though simply sharing a name with celebrated author L. M. Montgomery provided some impetus and inspiration in choosing a name for his house. But was there more to it? Was some member of Charles Montgomery's family a fan of the Anne series? The family did make a trip to enjoy the area around the Island's famed beaches in August 1914,[177] and repeated the excursion in 1915[178] and 1916.[179] Was the shared house name and surname a source of pride, or just a running joke with which some family connection was feigned with a wink and a nod? It may be impossible to ever know the answers to these questions, but it is not inconceivable that all of these ideas and more factored into Charles Montgomery's motivations, as a house name was often possessed of multi-layered meanings and associations.

L. M. Montgomery's books are of course filled with wonderful house names so beautifully suited to the fanciful nature of the narrative and wide-eyed curiosity of her young heroines. In *Emily of New Moon*, Montgomery's young protagonist ponders, "I like New Moon. It's so *stately* and *splendid* here.... And it seems as if we must be very aristokratik when we have a sun dyal."[180]

ST. EULALIE

Sunshine of St. Eulalie was she called, for that was the sunshine
Which, as the farmers believed, would load their orchards with apples.

—Henry Wadsworth Longfellow, *Évangéline*

St. Eulalie was the Grand Pré home of Sir Robert and Lady Weatherbe. Robert Weatherbe (1834–1915) attended Acadia College in Wolfville and went on to become a lawyer and Supreme Court judge.

St. Eulalie (or St. Eulalia) was a Spanish teenage girl who died a martyr for her convictions. She refused to recant her Christian beliefs even in the face of horrific torture. She miraculously survived being burned at the stake but was subjected to further tribulations before her torturers finished their work. "The Sequence of Saint Eulalia," also called "The Canticle of Saint Eulalia," is one of the oldest surviving texts of Old French. The text dates to about the year 880 and recounts the martyrdom of Eulalia in verse.

Évangéline, the Acadian heroine, was, in the opening pages of Longfellow's epic poem, a teenager not unlike Eulalie. The story of Évangéline begins in Grand-Pré where she is fondly referred to as the "Sunshine of St. Eulalie." And it was, as Longfellow goes on, that sunshine which the farmers believed would fill their orchards with apples.

As it turns out, Sir Robert's residence of *St. Eulalie* boasted such a magnificent orchard that tourists visiting the nearby old Covenanter Church had their attention diverted.[181] Indeed, in his later years, Sir Robert devoted a great deal of energy to advancing his estate. At the time of Robert's death in 1915, his apple orchard was said to be the largest in the province.[182] It would seem that the sunshine of St. Eulalie rewarded the gentleman farmer's faith with abundance.

MIZPAH COTTAGE

And Mizpah; for he said, The LORD watch between me and thee, when we are absent one from another.

—Genesis 31:49

Mizpah Cottage appears more frequently than one might expect for such a foreign-sounding name. The word *Mizpah* comes to us from the Bible. It has Hebrew origins and roughly translates as "watch tower." Although it appears a number of times in the Bible, the passage that is most likely the inspiration for naming a residence is Genesis 31:49, quoted above. Mizpah in this passage was the name given to a place where stones were gathered into a pillar to represent a covenant between God and two other parties: Jacob and his father-in-law, Laban. Mizpah, therefore, is a reference to a covenant between God and family members that the Lord will watch over them when they are separated and unable to watch over each other.

The name *Mizpah Cottage* is indicative of a Christian family who has one or more members called away for some purpose, be it to receive an education, pursue employment, engage in some form of service, or any other reason why life tends to separate people. The name *Mizpah Cottage* appears once in the Halifax area as well as in Lunenburg.

Mizpah Cottage, Lunenburg.

WAVERLEY

Sir Walter Scott (1771–1832) published his novel *Waverley* anonymously in 1814 to immediate success. This was the poet's first foray into prose fiction and is considered to be Western literature's first historical novel. The novel is set amid the Jacobite uprising of 1745. Protagonist Edward Waverley was raised on the family estate named *Waverley-Honour* and possesses family ties to both the Jacobite and Hanoverian sides.

In 1847, Charles P. Allen purchased seven hundred acres outside of Halifax. It was here that he made his home and manufactured furniture for the local market.[183] He called his estate *Waverley*, and the name was later adopted as the name of the community.[184] The novel *Waverley*, and subsequent works known collectively as the Waverley novels, are said to have been favourites of Charles P. Allen and the inspiration for naming his residence.[185]

Halifax had a *Waverley Cottage* on Windsor Street, the home of Frederick LeBlanc.[186]

Waverley, the estate, situated in what is now the community of the same name.

BLINK BONNIE COTTAGE

But a sight sae delightfu' I trow I ne'er spied
As the bonny blithe blink o' my ain fireside.

—Elizabeth Hamilton, "My Ain Fireside"

The name *Blink Bonnie Cottage* was given to a home in New Glasgow.[187] Additionally, the abridged name *Blink Bonnie* appears in Pictou,[188] Antigonish,[189] and Dartmouth,[190] and *Blinkbonnie* in Halifax.[191] The alliterative name with an unusual pairing of words has a Scottish origin that briefly means "glimpse of beauty." Its fully nuanced meaning, though, could be described as a glimpse of beauty so enchanting that it forever marks one with a longing to behold it, as if etched not just on one's memory but also on one's soul.

It is not known if the lines quoted above from Scottish author and poet Elizabeth Hamilton (1758–1816) served as the original or chief link between blink bonnie and the home, but the poem was widely known throughout the nineteenth century. Blink

Blink Bonnie, Antigonish.

bonnie as a general term or name saw regular usage in Scottish culture. As a name specifically for a residence it is easy to see its allure, being both descriptive and poetic. It was, and is, well-suited for an advantageously situated house with an attractive view whose inhabitants proudly profess their Scottish heritage.

FRIAR LAURENCE'S CELL

Hushed is the mirth of the banqueting hall;
The spider hath woven his woof from the wall,
Where graceful the folds of rich tapestry hung,
And where mirrors reflected the joyous and young.

—Charles Fenerty, "Passing Away"

Sir John Wentworth (1737–1820) had built for himself an estate at the head of the Bedford Basin, a site variously described at the time as six or seven miles from Halifax. He called his country mansion *Friar Laurence's Cell* in allusion to Shakespeare's *Romeo and Juliet*.[192]

Prince Edward, Duke of Kent (1767–1820), commander-in-chief of the forces in British North America, leased Wentworth's estate and enlarged the original house, transforming it into a two-storey Italian-style villa. Various ancillary buildings were

Painting of *Friar Laurence's Cell*, Prince's Lodge, Halifax.

erected and the grounds were extensively worked to produce a sylvan retreat for his beloved Julie, whose name it is believed, was written out in the form of a large garden path. It is unclear when exactly—whether during the prince's tenancy or shortly thereafter—the place became known as *Prince's Lodge*. There is also one source that identifies the estate as *Prince's Folly*,[193] though this was likely a colloquialism.

The original name, *Friar Laurence's Cell*, is most intriguing. It is not known why Wentworth chose the unusual name, but two possibilities stand out. The Shakespeare character, Friar Laurence, was the only trusted confidant of both Romeo and Juliet. Did Wentworth see himself as a trusted confidant? In *Romeo and Juliet*, the Friar's grounds boasted a wealth of herbs and flowers. Did Wentworth see himself as a keen horticulturalist?

The first possibility now seems strangely prophetic in that the forbidden relationship of Romeo and Juliet mirrors the impossible relationship of Edward and Julie. Julie St. Laurent was the Duke's mistress, a role disapproved of by his father, King George III.

The second possibility acknowledges Shakespeare's Friar Laurence as a sort of steward of a diverse stock of important plants. Wentworth held a somewhat similar post as Surveyor General of the King's Woods in North America, a role in which he scouted out and reserved for the king's navy all trees suitable for ships' masts.[194]

The real inspiration behind the name *Friar Laurence's Cell* may never be unearthed; as it stands, it is perhaps the most intriguing of all estate names in the province.

CLIFTON

No one ever seed as much dirt in my house as a fly couldn't brush off with his wings.

—Sam Slick in Thomas C. Haliburton's *The Clockmaker*

Clifton, a country villa, was built about 1833 for Thomas Chandler Haliburton, distinguished judge and author. Haliburton is perhaps best remembered for the sayings and doings of his fictional character, Sam Slick, made popular in his book *The Clockmaker*. It has been said that the name *Clifton* was chosen to commemorate the birthplace of Haliburton's wife, Louisa.[195] The assertion, however pervasive and plausible, does not appear in any primary documentation. Perhaps supporting evidence will yet turn up. In addition to *Clifton*, the estate has been variously known as *Clifton Cottage*, *Clifton House*, *Clifton Grove*, and the *Sam Slick House*.[196] The assortment is almost enough to make one pronounce that Slick-ism, "Six of one, half a dozen of the other"; however, some of the names originate from the property's time as a hotel. The *grove* suffix

Clifton, Windsor.

is quite understandable, as one of the defining characteristics of the estate was the four- to five-acre grove of trees with an additional two and a half acres of orchard.[197] The name *Sam Slick House* is certainly the odd one in the mix, not just because it discards Clifton altogether but because it appropriates the name of a fictional character. Though Sam Slick himself was not a particularly lovable character, the name *Sam Slick House* does possess an endearing quality that celebrates the author and his offbeat Yankee salesman.

SUNNY SIDE

...a little old-fashioned stone mansion, all made up of gable-ends, and as full of angles and corners as an old cocked hat.

—Washington Irving, *Chronicles of Wolfert's Roost*

It is impossible to say definitively where certain house names originated or when exactly it was that a homeowner first heard a name he thought would suit his grounds better than most. A name like *Sunny Side*, so ubiquitous and so generic, might have originated from any number of inspirations. In the absence of documentary evidence clearly recording why a family decided upon such a name, anecdotal details are the only means of exploring possible influences and inspirations. For *Sunny Side*, two such sources stand out. One is obvious: our love for the sun and our tendency to orient

Sunny Side, Dartmouth.

our homes toward a sunny southern exposure. The other, to be explored first, is the long-admired American estate of the same name.

Sunnyside, the Tarrytown, New York, estate of American author Washington Irving (1783–1859) was well known during much of Irving's life, and his house survives today as a museum. During the mid-nineteenth century Irving's *Sunnyside* appeared frequently in *Harper's Weekly*, Currier & Ives prints, and a local guidebook,[198] with the latter treating the estate as an unofficial tourist site. Irving's short stories "Rip Van Winkle" and the "Legend of Sleepy Hollow" are still well known today, but other works also earned him terrific fame throughout his career as an author. One of his works, *Chronicles of Wolfert's Roost*, took its name from Irving's estate, *Sunnyside*, which he informally and playfully nicknamed *Wolfert's Roost* in recognition of its former owner, Wolfert Acker. Irving purchased the idyllic Hudson River property from Acker in 1835 and soon after commenced a major expansion of the house and remodelling of the grounds. The book *Chronicles of Wolfert's Roost* was heavily promoted in Halifax at the time of its publication in 1855,[199] and the author opens the book with a history and description of his *Sunnyside* estate.

American author Oliver Wendell Holmes (1809–1894) declared that Irving's

Sunnyside stood "next to *Mount Vernon*, the best known and most cherished of all the dwellings in our land."[200] Landscape architect A. J. Downing praised the vine-clad *Sunnyside* as "the beau ideal of a cottage orné."[201]

So there is ample evidence to illustrate there was a high degree of renown for Irving's estate and a multitude of positive attributes that one might have associated with it. While there is nothing conclusive to suggest a link between Irving's *Sunnyside* and properties of the same name in Dartmouth[202] and Maitland[203], there is little doubt that the successful author popularized the name and occasioned widespread recognition of it, including here in Nova Scotia. The compound spelling, *Sunnyside*, was preferred by property owners in Onslow[204] and Truro.[205]

Setting aside the influence of a famous estate, a simple admiration for the sun, as already observed, may have been sufficient motivation for crafting a variety of house names founded on the sun theme. Even advice connected to health and wellness could elevate one's regard for the sun, as the good citizens of Digby discovered.

SUNNISIDE COTTAGE

The commandment forbids us to covet whatever belongs to our neighbor; but surely one may envy the sun his glorious rising in the east—his high and proud career, with all the splendor of his noon-day beams—and then his calm and dignified decline; his rays still lingering to brighten and adorn the clouds that hang around the world.

—Joseph Howe, quoted in M. G. Parks, ed., *Western and Eastern Rambles: Travel Sketches of Nova Scotia*

The people of Digby County were advised to cut down trees that were close enough to their houses to obscure the sun. They were told to allow the sun to flood every room in their house and to sunbathe every day. The sun will give colour and beauty to the complexion, they were told, but if one is forced to stay indoors all day, he should try to get near the sunny window where the sun's effects may still be felt. This was the wisdom imparted by the *Digby Weekly Courier* at the dawn of the twentieth century. The sun, citizens were told, "is so essential to our health and happiness that when it is taken away from us we become weak and pale. But when we go out in the warm sunlight again new strength and health come to us."[206] Within two years of this exaltation of the sun, the first documented use of *Sunniside Cottage*[207] can be found in Smiths Cove, Digby County.

This name and its Washington Irving variation, *Sunnyside*, were not the only appellations that esteemed a sunny situation. *Sunshine Cottage*[208] was located in Purcells Cove and *Sunnybank* could be found in Great Village.[209] Truro must have been seriously soliciting favours from old Sol as that town was not only home to the aforementioned *Sunnyside* but also had a *Sunny Side Cottage*[210] and a *Sunset Cottage*.[211]

BOSCOBEL

Old Pendrill, the miller, at the risk of his blood,
Hid the king of the isle in the king of the wood.

—An Old-English refrain in A. M. Broadley's *The Royal Miracle*, 1912

Boscobel, a property located at Jollimore on the Northwest Arm, shares a name with *Boscobel House* of Shropshire, England. The English *Boscobel House* is associated with the well-known story of the Royal Oak. This famous tree was located on the grounds of *Boscobel House*, and its story was at one time familiar to every schoolboy.[212] The story of the Royal Oak begins after the Battle of Worcester in 1651, when Charles II fled from Cromwell's soldiers with the aid of Charles Giffard and Francis Yates. The fugitive sovereign cut his hair, dirtied his face, and was disguised as a common woodman by the Penderel family, tenants of the Giffards at *Boscobel*. After feeling the house might be unsafe as a refuge, the king was led out to the surrounding woods. While hiding in Boscobel Wood, the king is said to have climbed an oak tree before one of Cromwell's soldiers passed below him. Francis Yates was executed for his role in Charles's escape. The story of Charles and the life-saving oak became popular after the Restoration in 1660, and the tree attained renown with the establishment of Royal Oak Day (also

Boscobel, Northwest Arm, Halifax.

known as Oak Apple Day), still celebrated in England. The oak, the monarch of the forest, came to signify loyalty to the throne.

Boscobel on the Northwest Arm takes its name from the story of the Royal Oak. Henry C. D. Twining (1820–1886), owner of *Boscobel*, is believed to be descended from the heroic Francis Yates through his mother, Susan Winniett.[213]

RAVENSWOOD

When the last Laird of Ravenswood to Ravenswood shall ride
and woo a dead maiden to be his bride,
He shall stable his steed in the Kelpie's flow,
And his name shall be lost for evermore!

—Sir Walter Scott, *The Bride of Lammermoor*, 1819

Ravenswood was said to have been named for Sir Walter Scott's hero, Edgar, Master of Ravenswood in *The Bride of Lammermoor*, first published in 1819.[214] In the romantic tragedy, Edgar's father is stripped of the family's *Ravenswood* estate for his support of the deposed King James VII. When Sir William Ashton purchases the estate, Edgar sees the

Ravenswood, Dutch Village Road, Halifax.

Ashton family as usurpers of his family's inheritance, resulting in a high degree of enmity. Edgar later unwittingly saves the life of young Lucy Ashton and the pair fall in love. The romantic development melts any earlier resentment between Edgar and Sir William, but the villainous Lady Ashton vows to sabotage any union between the young romantics.

The novel contains elements of the supernatural, which is noteworthy in that stories of hauntings were also connected with Halifax's *Ravenswood*.[215]

HEBRON HOUSE

So all the elders of Israel came to the king at Hebron; and King David made a league with them in Hebron before the LORD: and they anointed David king over Israel.

—2 Samuel 5:3

Anthony Landers began hosting Methodist meetings in his Yarmouth County residence called *Hebron House* in 1810. Seven years later, he had a chapel constructed in the vicinity.[216] Landers extended the name Hebron Corner to the general area around *Hebron House*, much of which he owned. The name was eventually shortened to Hebron.[217] Rev. John R. Campbell, who authored a history of Yarmouth County in 1876, gives much credit to Landers for introducing and advancing Methodism in this locality.[218] As an ardent supporter of Methodism, Landers would have been familiar with Biblical references to ancient Hebron in Palestine. The city of Hebron was the Old Testament location where Abraham and much of his family were buried. It is also the site of David's anointing as king. Whether as a house name or a place name, *Hebron*, a Hebrew word meaning "united" or "friendship," possesses a pleasant and appropriate association.

DAY SPRING COTTAGE

May God be gracious to us and bless us and make his face shine on us.
—Psalm 67:1

Day Spring Cottage in Dartmouth was situated on the Shore Road. It possessed a splendid view of the harbour entrance.[219] Beyond the harbour, the first rays of the rising sun could be seen each morning on the horizon. Day spring, or dayspring, is a poetic term for daybreak or the dawning of the light. Its use is most often associated with the

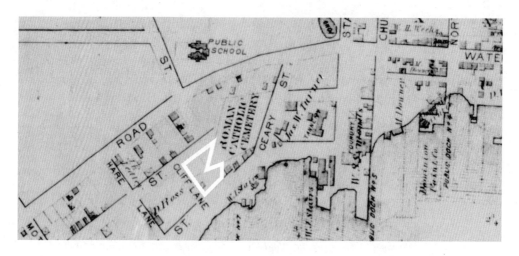

Day Spring Cottage, Dartmouth, on 1878 Hopkins-Vandervoort map of Dartmouth.

Bible where it appears in several books. The term's strong association with the Bible indicates that *Day Spring Cottage* was likely named with more than just a fond affection for sunrises and that the name was likely chosen to remind the home's inhabitants of the glory of the Lord shining down on all God's people.

MANTUA AND CREMONA

Yon light is not day-light, I know it, I:
It is some meteor that the sun exhales,
To be to thee this night a torch-bearer,
And light thee on thy way to Mantua:
Therefore stay yet; thou need'st not to be gone.

—William Shakespeare, *Romeo and Juliet*

John Day (d.1775) purchased land near Newport, Hants County, in 1765. It is unclear whether Day named the property *Mantua* or if some earlier resident had bestowed the honour. Whoever deserves the credit obviously possessed some knowledge of the Italian city of the same name. Mantua, Italy, was the town nearest the birthplace of the poet Virgil and the place where Shakespeare's Romeo had been banished. It had been a renowned centre of arts and culture, not just in Italy, but throughout all of Europe for hundreds of years.

The estate, *Mantua*, Hants County.

Mantua, Italy, may have been favoured by artists, but it was no pantywaist militarily. The city occupied a strong defensive position, being almost entirely surrounded by water, and history shows it was not easily entered by unfriendly powers. The Mincio River, with its associated lakes, encloses the city in a protective mantle on three sides. This geographic advantage bears a remarkable resemblance to the seven hundred acres of land belonging to John Day of Hants County.[220] Like the Mincio River of Italy, the St. Croix, with its tributary Herbert, wraps itself around Day's lands and that similarity must have been a contributing factor in naming the place. A look at historic records reveals the parallels are actually far more blatant: the Herbert River actually bore the name Mincio River for a time.

Another nearby residence, carved out of lands originally belonging to *Mantua*, was owned by the Woolaver family and named *Cremona*. Cremona is also an Italian city, not far from Mantua.

THE PRIORY

But I live for the most part in a cottage outside of the town, where I can be secluded and free from observation....It is an old-fashioned wooden structure which they call The Priory.

—James De Mille, *Cord and Creese*

"I DID NOT MAKE ANY REPLY, BUT TOOK MY CREMONA, AND SOUGHT TO LIFT UP ALL MY SOUL TO A LEVEL WITH HERS."

After identifying some residences that took inspiration from literature, it is time to flip the concept and point out a Nova Scotia estate that appeared in a published work. A former Dalhousie University professor and accomplished author James De Mille wrote *Cord and Creese* (1869). The work of fiction contains a reference (see opening quote) to *The Priory*, near Halifax's Northwest Arm in 1847. The real-world *Priory* was the residence of Edward Pryor and situated on the north side of Jubilee Road. It is believed to have been destroyed by fire about 1870.[221] The name *priory*, which generally would refer to a religious house such as a monastery, is presumably derived from the family name. Interestingly, De Mille's wife, Elizabeth, was a Pryor.[222]

An illustration from James De Mille's *Cord and Creese*, 1871 edition.

Chapter 6

The PECULIAR
and UNIQUE

While most house names are derived from things that are dear to us—our family heritage, a chosen vocation, or even a favourite book—some house names aren't created from such thoughtful or deliberate motivations. Some house names come about much more organically or even by accident. The first chapter of this book explained the prevailing suffixes employed in house naming; each successive chapter attempts to identify some common inspirations. All of this makes the house-naming tradition appear somewhat formulaic and equips the reader with enough basic familiarity with the custom to jump right in and create a contemporary name for his or her own home. This chapter defies the conventions. This chapter collects some of the oddities and illustrates that even though it is tempting to try to condense the tradition down to a handy formula, in practice, the tradition can be much more individualistic and capricious than it first appears.

Swastika Cottage, Halifax, was named before the erstwhile good-luck symbol was appropriated and stigmatized by Nazi Germany. *Enola Cottage*, Halifax, has unknown origins, but its backward spelling of *alone* hints at some possible connection to concealment or solitude.

This chapter covers a diversity of naming origins that range from clever wordplay, to odd situations, and even to places that arrived at their names via more circuitous routes. One of the most endearing of the latter variety is *The Ghost House*.

THE GHOST HOUSE

And the death-bound frenzy of those gaunt trees
Still made an appeal to earth's sympathies,
While the lichens, white as a veteran's beard,
Made the withered spectres still more weird.

—Cassie Fairbanks, "The Lone House," Halifax, 1859

The Ghost House, North River, Colchester County.

When Mr. Will Smith purchased a well-known haunted house in Colchester County's community of North River, the year was 1906. Smith was well aware of the home's long-standing reputation; in fact, everyone had known the residence as "the Ghost House" for some time. *The Ghost House* was the perennial destination of choice for those taken up with Halloween revelry and an urge to frighten themselves on an annual basis. Whatever spooky encounters had earned the home its name, Smith was unconcerned, for he had designs on purchasing a picturesque summer home and he had found a deserted, though attractive place nestled in a grove of trees along the banks of a lovely river. The place was "one of the prettiest sites imaginable" with an "extensive view up the river and across the low lands to town that is exceedingly fine."[223] What was he to do with the home's notoriety and its unsettling moniker that was likely to linger even with a formal name change? Embrace it of course!

The local newspaper reported, "We are glad to learn that the now historic name of the place, 'Ghost House,' is not to be sacrificed for any modern, sentimental, hifalutin appendage." The account continued with proud approval, "It is the 'Ghost House' and the 'Ghost House' it will remain, though any Spirits, that hereafter may be around, will be of a different nature from those that heretofore were said to have floated about this lovely, lonely, deserted country manor."[224]

Not long after Smith had transformed the old house into a "handsome suburban cottage" the local newspaper could not contain its astonishment: "one could hardly imagine that around it a few years ago we were trying to find the habitat of a ghost or to pierce the visionary nothingness in which these disembodied spirits roam about."[225]

A final point regarding *The Ghost House* that begs comment is the 1906 newspaper quote that makes reference to "modern, sentimental" and "hifalutin" appendages. This wonderful and incredibly rare insight alludes to a sentiment of pretension on the part of the journalist with respect to those who name their properties—not that they altogether disapprove of the practice but that the giving of a name need not always reflect a stuffy, formal image. The writer conveys an almost tangible sense of being refreshed by Smith's unwillingness to put on airs.

TOTTEN RECTORY

Said to be one of the earliest houses erected in Digby, *Totten Rectory* was not always *Totten Rectory*. In fact, the house arrived at both its namesake and even its location in Digby rather circuitously. The house began its life in New York, where Commissary Haight, a Loyalist, dismantled it and brought the frame to Digby. "The timbers, which were 11 inches by 6, were placed perpendicularly, close together, and must have been intended to resist attack." Haight apparently wanted a robust structure that would be bulletproof. Haight's secure Digby home became the lodging of choice for the Duke of Kent whenever he visited Digby. The room in which the prince stayed became known as the "Prince's Room."[226]

Before his death, Commissary Haight willed the property to his only child, Agnes, and if she died without heirs, the house was to go to his good friend Nancy Totten. Agnes married Colonel Hatfield, but the couple's only child died in infancy. Following Agnes's death, Nancy Totten took possession.[227]

Totten must have been grateful for the solid, fortress-like construction, for she soon found herself living under a state of siege. Doors and windows were said to have been barred as the Hatfield relatives pressed *their* case for inheritance. Totten was steadfast, and eventually the title challenge was dropped. Upon her death, the property passed to the Church of England as per her wishes.[228]

For many years, Trinity Anglican Church used the house as a rectory and so it was named *Totten Rectory*.[229] In 1890, while under the care of one Reverend Doctor Ambrose, the rectory was destroyed by fire.

OCTAGON TERRACE

There is something about an eight-sided building that causes people to pause and marvel at its form. Wonder and awe shape one's thoughts. How is the interior laid out? What is it like to live there? Dartmouth's *Octagon Terrace*, also called *Octagon House*, was built in 1871 and demolished in 1969. The original owner, Gavin Holliday, only resided in the place for several years before leaving Dartmouth altogether. Successive owners took up residence, and at some point the appearance of the house was likened to an ink bottle.

Ink Bottle House is another name by which this property became known,[230] although whether the name was designated by owners or colloquially applied by neighbours is unclear. The nickname *Ink Bottle* is often applied to octagon houses as the almost trademark form of the dispenser was also eight-sided with the neck of the bottle approximating the cupola that generally adorns octagon houses and barns.

The name *Octagon Terrace* obviously suits the house as well as any name can, but it also reconciles itself to the grounds that echoed the house's unique shape in the form of a terraced octagon. If one were to go further in contemplating how wonderfully suited *Octagon Terrace* was to its surroundings, it could also be pointed out that, from the air, the house on Dahlia Street exhibited the same circular perfection as a dahlia.

Octagon Terrace, Dartmouth.

MAROON HALL

Maroon Hall was situated on an elevation in Preston that offered extensive views of the surrounding countryside. During the first half of the nineteenth century, *Maroon Hall* was the summer home of several prominent owners who, in their turn, hosted dinners and dances for the entertainment of the fashionable men and women of Halifax society.[231] This spirited and sociable atmosphere was actually a revival of an earlier raison d'être when the house was periodically appropriated by the Maroons, a band of several hundred African-Jamaicans relocated to Preston in 1796, and ultimately Sierra Leone in 1800.

The Maroons would assemble at *Maroon Hall*, as it was then called,[232] for dances and other merriment, which they proudly attended in their West Indian finery. The hall itself was a two-storey, forty-by-forty-foot structure that was home to Col. W. D. Quarell and Alexander Ochterlony, superintendents of the Maroon settlement. The house had actually been built as a summer home a few years previously but was purchased along with considerable other lands to facilitate Maroon resettlement—much of which was funded by the Jamaican government.

A room in *Maroon Hall* was used as a chapel and school and it was in this room where the black gentry and their wives would hold their entertainment.[233] After an auction of government-held Preston properties in 1801, *Maroon Hall* was returned to private hands and successive owners retained its historic name until fire claimed it in 1856.[234] A smaller dwelling bearing the same name replaced the original *Maroon Hall*. During their short stay, the Maroons also left their name at Halifax Citadel, where they volunteered their labour to build Maroon Bastion.[235]

THE STONEHOUSE

"Welcome to Dingley Farm, Joe," said Mrs. Wood, with her jolly laugh, as she watched me jump from the carriage seat to the ground....

"Aunt Hattie, why is the farm called Dingley Farm?" said Miss Laura, as she went into the house. "It ought to be Wood Farm."

"Dingley is made out of 'dingle,' Laura. You know that pretty hollow back of the pasture? It is what they call a 'dingle.' So this farm was called Dingle Farm till the people around about got saying 'Dingley' instead. I suppose they found it easier."

—Marshall Saunders, *Beautiful Joe*

Located in Heatherton, near the forks of the Pomquet River, *The Stonehouse* is one of those peculiar house names that breaks with convention. The name is one that was

The Stonehouse, right, Heatherton, Antigonish County.

neither thoughtfully selected by the owner nor was it particularly descriptive. You see, *Stonehouse* is built of wood. This wooden version, however, did replace an earlier stone structure also known by the same name. In 1900, the last owner of the stone structure, Duncan A. Chisholm, had the house torn down because it had gained an unwholesome association with causing sickness. The sturdy four-foot-thick walls were difficult to dismantle for R. A. MacDonald, the Black Avon man, who assisted with razing the house. Stubborn, too, was the name itself, *Stonehouse*. For even after building a new wood-framed dwelling, locals still called the property the *Stonehouse*.

Duncan himself could not escape the name. As often happened in this part of Nova Scotia, with just a handful of distinct surnames and oft-repeated first names, residents regularly attached an additional descriptor to someone's given name, particularly if that name was common. So, Duncan Chisholm was known as "Duncan Stonehouse," despite having no apparent love for the former wayside landmark that was blamed for casting debilitating effects on its inhabitants. In the end, Duncan did not have long to enjoy his salubrious new abode. Ill health plagued him and despite seeking respite in the dry climate of New Mexico, Duncan died in 1907 at the young age of forty.[236] Successive owners of the wood-framed *Stonehouse* have had little choice but to accept the misnomer.

WINCKWORTH

The *Winckworth* estate was listed for sale in the *Royal Gazette*, April 1, 1800.

Winckworth Tonge (c. 1727–1792) was an Irishman and a member of the British Army. Among other assignments, he saw action at the sieges of Louisbourg in 1758 and of Quebec in 1759. By the time of the American Revolution, his military role had diminished to militia service—though in this he held the rank of colonel. The House of Assembly saw him represent several county seats during a lengthy political career, while perhaps his foremost role was that of naval officer, an influential occupation that oversaw shipping in the colony.[237] During his varied levels of service to the Crown he had acquired land. A considerable portion of this was in Hants County, amounting to about two thousand acres nestled between Windsor and St. Croix. This he called *Winckworth*.

Now, it is not often one names his estate after his own first name but *Winckworth* is typically a surname, and it is probable that Winckworth Tonge had a maternal connection of some distinction to the name. Wentworth Road, today an important artery connecting Windsor and Sweets Corner, reveals a corruption of this early estate name.[238]

Alexander Brymer (1745–1822) succeeded Tonge as owner of the *Winckworth* estate. By the year 1800, he was selling *Winckworth* and preparing to return to England. A description of the property at that time reveals a mansion house and six leased cottages situated on a navigable river with dyked marshland, cleared uplands, and woodlands.[239]

FOREST COTTAGE AND ADAMS HOUSE

Some places, it seems, cultivate a keen sense of wit. Maybe it's the environment or the culture, or maybe it's just as simple as one jokester trying to outdo another. New Glasgow was (and perhaps still is) one of those places.

What would a gentleman call his house if his surname was Underwood? Well, if he lived in New Glasgow and he was a merchant by the name of George W. Underwood, he would, of course, live at *Forest Cottage*.[240]

Not to be outdone, there was a house on Provost Street in New Glasgow bearing the notice "'Adams House:' a little higher up is eaves."

TOWER HOUSE

The dominant architectural feature of the "large and commodious" house is a tower—and a massive one at that. The tower's bulk is out of all proportion to the rest of the house and its mass is unbalanced with any other architectural feature associated with the structure. The massing of forms of *Tower House* effectively diminishes as one's eyes move from the tower to each contiguous bay and addition, until one reaches the tiny covered porch at the far end. But this is how the great medieval tower houses of Europe tended to be: a single massive tower dwarfing the attached structures, albeit this Halifax tower house is constructed of wood, not stone.

Unlike its stone antecedents, *Tower House* was not built for defensive purposes. The uppermost level terminates in a decorative belvedere rather than defensive parapets. The owner was Colonel Bennet Henderson Hornsby,[241] a native of Kentucky, who fought for the Confederate Army in the American Civil War, following which he moved to Nova Scotia. The house sat on a single-acre lot on Edinburgh Street, Willow Park, Halifax, and is said to have had a large entrance hall, library, dining and drawing rooms, and four airy and lofty bedrooms.[242]

CLAREMONT

Clarence H. Dimock of Windsor resided at *Claremont*.[243] *Claremont* is a short-form of Mount Clarence; and so, it appears that this name followed the egocentric genus of the house-naming tradition. Apart from vanity, though, the name *Claremont* had another interesting association. The name was well-known in Victorian times as a royal residence in the county of Surrey. Queen Victoria visited many times, beginning in her youth when her doting uncle, Leopold, feted her with magical birthday celebrations and later in adulthood when the same uncle loaned her the estate. Victoria later bought *Claremont* for her fourth son, also named Leopold, upon the prince's marriage in 1882.[244] C. H. Dimock's inference to living on a large, well-manicured, royal estate was likely not intended as another heap of egotistical bombast but as a droll allusion, effectively tempering the vanity associated with naming his house after himself.

Aftermath of the 1897 fire that destroyed *Claremont* and much of Windsor.

THE GRAY HOUSE

The Gray House, left, Annapolis Royal, c. 1880.

Painted grey and inhabited by the Gray family, someone in *The Gray House* must have admired tongue-in-cheek humour. With a resident jokester, the disposition of this Annapolis Royal house must have been anything but grey. Sadly though, there was one dismal day in 1886 when this cheerful house was lost to fire.[245]

KELPIE LODGE

Come, ye Nymphs and Water sprites,
All ye Mermaids of the sea,
Min'sters of the Classic rites,
Of Historic Arcadie.

—D. M. Matheson, "Chebucto," 1916

In the late nineteenth and early twentieth centuries, Digby County was a summer resort destination. Wealthy and influential people, many of them American, swelled the communities surrounding Annapolis Basin.[246] One of them was Rev. Thomas A. Jaggar (1839–1912), bishop of the Diocese of Southern Ohio. Bishop Jaggar bought a point of land at Smiths Cove, and at some juncture he gave it the curious name *Kelpie Lodge*.[247] Here, the musician, painter, and outdoorsman would come to seek solace for a weak psychological constitution, in connection with which he once sadly remarked, "When mind and spirit fail, there is no help."[248]

A kelpie is a mythological sea creature, a water spirit often associated with the lochs of Scotland, sometimes possessing the body of a horse, and bent on either drowning or saving people from drowning. St. Columba is said to have banished a kelpie at Loch Ness in the year 565 for the creature having taken a man's life. Bishop Jaggar liked to hunt and fish, but it is unlikely that he fancied himself a modern-day St. Columba perched on the shore of a loch in *New* Scotland. Still, the connection between kelpies and drownings marks a tragic event and its proximity to *Kelpie Lodge* as an extraordinary coincidence.

On August 4, 1904, tragedy occurred in calm waters just below the bishop's home. In broad daylight, a small yacht of American tourists and several locals returning to shore had become grounded on a bar, upon which at low tide it was possible to walk ashore just above the bishop's. Rather than wait for rising waters to lift the yacht, it appears the occupants endeavoured to continue on their way aboard the yacht's too-small tender, with the result that the skiff capsized and seven people drowned. The captain, a seasoned sailor and member of the yacht club, was among those lost. It was supposed that he may have been pressured by his charges to get them to their destination at Bear River Station and overloaded the skiff against his better judgement.[249]

It is not known why Jaggar named his summer residence *Kelpie Lodge*, but the fatal accident that played out off Jaggars Point makes the tragedy an eerily prescient event.

TRIANGLE COTTAGE

Nova Scotia has had its share of odd-shaped architecture in the form of octagon structures, round buildings, flat-iron properties, and even its own Pentagon Building. Should the province not have a triangle cottage also? Well, this name is rather misleading: it doesn't actually refer to the shape of the house; it refers to the shape of a one-acre lot in mid-nineteenth century Halifax. *Triangle Cottage* was the property of John Steele that included a square house, two small barns, and a garden.[250] It occupied the land between two converging roads, Kempt Road and the old Windsor Road.

IONIC COTTAGE

Built on Gottingen Street in Halifax, the *Ionic Cottage* was also known by its more formal appellation, the *Grecian Ionic Cottage*. It is an unusual name for a property for a couple of reasons. First, is the incongruous nature of the name, as we tend not to imagine cottage design following the strict rules of classical architecture that this name implies. The Ionic order is one of the three orders of classical architecture, Doric and Corinthian being the other two. The Ionic order is characterized by the slender Ionic column, which is topped by a capital consisting of volutes, or scroll ornamentation. The other unusual aspect of the name is the austere, unemotional response that it conveys, which contrasts with the warm, homey, or even personal nuances of most names.

Though the *Ionic Cottage* is not alone in house names derived from architectural style, another similar derivation, *The Bungalow*, possessed connotations of relaxation and *savoir faire* in its early days. Such favourable emotions or associations actually made *The Bungalow* a popular house name in the early twentieth century.

Chapter 7

VOCATIONS
and IDENTITY

❦

A good many estate names are intimately connected to occupation and lifestyle: the sea captain who resides at *The Anchorage*, the minister at *The Hermitage*, or the soldier at *The Bivouac* all seem so suitably sheltered. Occupations sometimes inconveniently claim so much of who we are; yet, their contribution to identity also has affirming and self-respecting components. And so, it is those positive associations that induce and inspire house names connected to vocations.

Ministers all lived in named homes, though most of these followed the predictable formula of their respective Christian denomination, being known as *The Parsonage*, *The Rectory, The Manse*, or *The Glebe*. Occasionally, a slightly more individualized name such as the *Methodist Parsonage* could be found. *Acadia Manse,*[251] which cannot be ignored for its tongue-in-cheek phonetic similarity to its home community of Acadia Mines (Londonderry), was the home of Rev. W. A. Ross. Use of the name *The Vicarage* is rare but has been noted in Falmouth[252] and Truro.[253] Its use in both cases was associated with Anglican ministers.

Church closures or unions could result in a minister's home being deemed surplus and sold. In such instances, it was not uncommon for the residence to retain the respectable title of *Manse* or *Parsonage* even after being sold and no longer owned by the church.

THE HERMITAGE

And the unbark'd logs which that squatter hew'd
Still form the walls of that cabin rude.

—Cassie Fairbanks, *The Lone House*, 1859

CHURCH WORK.

We speak concerning Christ and the Church.

A Monthly Pamphlet of Facts, Notes and Instruction.

Vol. XXIII.   MIDDLE SACKVILLE, HALIFAX CO., NOV., 1898.   No. 9

REV. JOHN AMBROSE, M.A., D.C.L.

Rev. John Ambrose, sketched here, lived in *The Hermitage*.

Rev. John Ambrose (1823–1898) did not follow the predictable practice of calling his residence *The Rectory*, although the name of his home in Middle Sackville did beautifully befit his calling. This man of the cloth's residence was known as *The Hermitage*.[254] A hermitage is defined as a secluded residence or retreat; an alternate meaning indicates it may be associated with a hermit. For Reverend Ambrose then, *The Hermitage* was a highly suitable name for its link to poverty and humility—two attributes often associated with a life of serving the Lord. Reverend Ambrose was devoted to improving the lives of those in poverty. While in charge of the parish of Digby, he secured the abolition of the inhuman system of selling paupers to the lowest bidder—a practice then in vogue in the Maritimes.[255]

The Hermitage name could also be found in North Sydney,[256] Truro,[257] and Halifax. *The Hermitage* in Halifax was where the Armitage family lived.[258] If you think the surname Armitage sounds suspiciously like hermitage you might be beginning to understand how this quirky house-naming thing works. The surname Armitage is said to originate in eastern England and be derived from Hermitage, which is also one of several alternate spellings of the name.

Though it carries a connotation of modesty, *The Hermitage* is a name that is famous for some splendidly opulent houses, including the home of Andrew Jackson, seventh president of the United States, and a palace in St. Petersburg, Russia, with connections to Catherine the Great.

Norway House, Pictou, c. 1912.

NORWAY HOUSE

Is this an odd name for a residence with no direct connection to Scandinavia? Not if you're proud of your business acumen and record seventy-five-year tenure with the historic Hudson's Bay Company. Beginning as an apprentice clerk about 1838, the Scottish-born Donald Alexander Smith (1820–1914) rose to become governor and principal shareholder in the company, while simultaneously dabbling in a myriad of other leading companies as well as provincial and federal politics.[259] For many years, the Hudson's Bay Company's most important interior trading post was called *Norway House*, located in present-day Manitoba.

The original trading post at *Norway House* was constructed in 1817 by a group of Norwegian labourers, said to be ex-convicts. As if to underscore the importance of this post at the top of Lake Winnipeg, the Hudson's Bay Company actually held its annual meetings there for nearly half a century. The meetings consisted of planning decisions for the following year and management promotion. So, it was at *Norway House* that Smith finally ascended to governor of the company, and it was the significance of the place in his professional life that provided inspiration in naming his stately Pictou, Nova Scotia, residence, which was constructed of cut stone. Sir Donald Smith is also remembered for the honour of having driven the last spike on the Canadian Pacific Railway.

BACHELOR'S HALL

Oh, Bachelor's Hall it is always the best,
Be you sick, drunk, or sober you are always at rest;
No wife for to scold you, no children to bawl;
Oh, happy's the man that keeps Bachelor's Hall.

—Kenneth Peacock, *Songs of the Newfoundland Outports*, vol. 1, 1965

The use of the catchy refrain above, or variations of it, can be dated at least as far back as 1896 in Nova Scotia,[260] but it certainly goes back well before that as an 1897 quote implies: "Cook's Brook can yet boast of three residents, who are firm believers in the old ballad, 'The Bachelor's Hall is one of the best.'"[261]

Bachelor's Hall was a label often informally bestowed on a residence inhabited by one or more single men. The name appears to have been so commonly used as a running joke that it is difficult to tell in which instances it was used as jest and in which instances the inhabitant had actually assumed and accepted the moniker. Acceptance, though, was never in doubt when it came to a similarly named house in Cape Breton.

A North Sydney home, proudly known as *The Bachelors*, a play on the popular form used in the house-naming tradition (*The Maples*, *The Oaks*, and so on) was the residence of five single men. Now, in case anyone thought this was some sort of party house or forerunner to a latter-day man cave, they could be assured that any events

View of Court House Hill, Bible Hill, c. 1900, site of *Bachelor's Hall*.

associated with the residence were very much on the up and up. In 1903, an "efficiently chaperoned" whist party was held at *The Bachelors* where the ladies' first prize was a handsome cut-glass bowl and the gentleman's first prize, a silver-mounted hat brush.[262]

A Bible Hill house named *Bachelors' Hall* was home to some eight or ten young men—lawyers, doctors, and merchants. These young men were noted for their pranks and youthful frolics while living together, but many afterwards achieved distinction as men of substance.[263]

Of course, being a bachelor doesn't have to be a life-long calling. If some determined lady seizes upon the leap year tradition or if a man overcomes his bashfulness what then becomes of the name *Bachelor's Hall*? A. L. Goodwin, erstwhile bachelor at Landor, Colchester County, found out. The local newspaper announced that his house since being occupied by a newly married couple was not a *Bachelor's Hall* any longer.[264]

THE ANCHORAGE

The Anchorage, on the shores of Darling Lake near Yarmouth, was a place that Captain Aaron Churchill built for his family to escape the summer heat of the south. Churchill went to sea at age fourteen and, when still in his teens, got the nickname "Rudder" during a harrowing voyage in which the ship's rudder had to be replaced several times. After moving to Georgia, the Yarmouth native made his fortune in shipping and stevedoring but returned to Nova Scotia to enjoy his summers at *The Anchorage*, his appropriately named mansion.[265]

The Anchorage, Yarmouth.

SAWDUST RETREAT

Thomas Gotobed McMullen resided in Truro at *The Cedars*, a palatial residence built in 1891. Known widely as "the lumber king," he engaged in extensive forestry operations throughout much of Nova Scotia with complementary interests in ships and rails. His son, Frank A. McMullen (1870–1941), managed a sawmill in Hants County.[266] Being a "chip off the old block" (of wood), he named his home in South Maitland *Sawdust Retreat*. Local newspapers kept pace with the busy family, often printing briefs similar to this one from 1898: "Mr. Frank McMullen left 'Sawdust Retreat,' South Maitland, yesterday, was at the 'Cedars' last night, and returned home today."[267] In 1898, three young lady visitors, one likely a niece, stayed at the house for ten days, and, despite the overtly industrial attributes of the name, were thoroughly charmed. The girls were said to have come away from the place with a better understanding of "Sawdust's" "potent power to move the stubborn heart."[268]

HOLMWORTH

Hon. Rev. Burnthorn Musgrave's residence *Holmworth* in Auburn took on new meaning when his daughters decided to open a home school in the family home. The Misses Musgrave called the venture Holmworth English Home School.

Holmworth, Auburn, Kings County, c. 1900.

THE GRANGE

A grange is a British word that may be used to describe the country house and associated buildings of a gentleman farmer. Thomas Ritchie (1777–1852), lawyer, judge, and politician, resided in Annapolis Royal at "that well known and very desirable property" known as *The Grange*. An 1864 description of the homestead reveals that it was a large and airy house of twelve rooms, not including cellar, kitchens, and attic. The property also boasted good stables, coach houses, and other outbuildings. The garden was "beautifully situated and tastefully laid out." Choice fruit trees of every description were located nearby with an orchard of valuable grafted stock in a high state of cultivation. Additional farm houses, barns, and cattle sheds rounded out the buildings connected to the agricultural work of the property's dyked marsh, pasture, and woodland.[269]

Though farming was not his primary or even secondary calling, Thomas Ritchie possessed first-hand knowledge of its challenges. As a member of the House of Assembly he guided farm loan legislation through the House in 1819.[270] An impressive working farm such as this was really an expression of the judge's station in life; indeed, it was said that "Annapolis belonged to Judge Ritchie, the church and the devil."[271]

The Grange, Annapolis Royal, c. 1890.

One of these humble dwellings is believed to be *Magazine Cottage*, Halifax.

MAGAZINE COTTAGE

Magazine Cottage was located near Her Majesty's Dockyard, on Campbell Road in Halifax. It was home to Hugh Morris, who was employed at the ordnance depot at the close of the nineteenth century.[272]

BALLARAT COTTAGE

A salute was fired on July 12, 1852, as the brig *Sebim* got under way, leaving Halifax for Australia. The journey, a well-planned scheme to settle in a distant land, had been hatched by several Doane brothers from Barrington and a number of their close friends, including Haligonian John F. Gabriel.[273] Their destination was Ballarat, Australia, a little-known sheep run that had seen its population explode over the previous year as gold fever induced prospectors to come from all quarters. In his mid-twenties, John was young enough to meet head-on the challenges of dwelling under canvas in the muddied, honeycombed landscape known as "the diggings" or "the gravel pits."

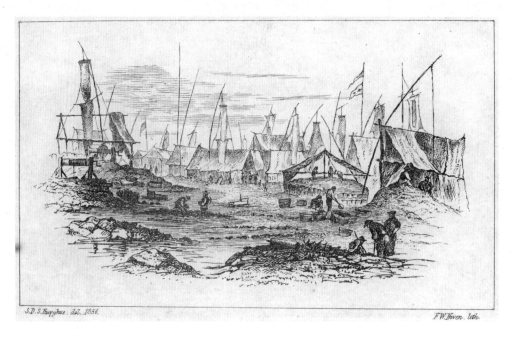

The Gravel Pits, Ballarat, Australia, 1854, by S. D. S. Huyghue.

Following John Gabriel's movements so many years later is not easy, but he must have returned to Nova Scotia within several years as, he popped up once more in Halifax in 1859, seemingly preparing for another lengthy excursion. At this point he owned a house in Halifax, opposite the Garrison Chapel, that he hoped to let before leaving. At the same time, he was trying to sell a recently constructed residence on the post road in Falmouth that he called *Ballarat Cottage*.[274] By this time, *Ballarat* was a name known the world over, for on June 9, 1858, the largest nugget then discovered—an astonishing 152 pounds—was hauled out of a Ballarat mine!

The auriferous land of Australia called John back, where he is said to have amassed considerable means in the gold fields.[275] By 1878, he was found prospecting in the remote coastal region of New Zealand called Big Bay. One day, he and several others loaded up their blunt tools and made a boat trip up the coast to visit a black-smith but never returned. The boat and its five passengers were lost. A couple of weeks later, John's crayfish-eaten body was found still in its miner's boots.[276]

HAYFIELD

Alexander Knight (1795–1873) was a saddler and harness maker, the same occupation of his father in Scotland, and of his son in Halifax. Alexander's son, William, took over his father's business upon the elder Knight's retirement in 1860.[277] Although it is not known if the primary encouragement for naming *Hayfield*[278] originated with the long-time paternal trade, there is nonetheless an obvious and pleasing association.

An ad for William F. Knight's saddlery and harness business as it appeared in *McAlpine's Halifax City Directory, 1872–73.*

SHERBROOKE COTTAGE

Under Your Excellency a system of education has been provided for those whose claims the benevolence of the community has overlooked. To your Excellency's liberal views we in this district owe the prosperity of a Seminary for the higher branches of learning, equally accessible to all denominations of Christians.

—Rev. Thomas McCulloch, 1816, from William McCulloch,
The Life of Thomas McCulloch, D. D.

Rev. Dr. Thomas McCulloch left Scotland in 1803 and arrived as a missionary in the fledgling colonial town of Pictou late that same year. The insufficient settlement consisted of some fourteen houses with the remainder of the Presbyterian congregation scattered throughout the wilderness. The minister and his family crammed into

Sherbrooke Cottage, Pictou.

existing, though wanting, quarters during their first few years. McCulloch's eventual home, finished in 1806, is notable for its brick construction in a place that generally favoured wood or stone. The learned reverend, who upon arrival was immediately esteemed for his possession of two globes, soon recognized the need to secure some form of higher learning for the young men of his charge. Thoughts soon morphed into a loftier vision: a future seminary.

The political climate of the day was tainted by sectarian prejudices, and McCulloch was forced to take small steps. He began by building the "log college" at the northwest corner of his property. After suspected incendiarism, he built a replacement structure east of his house.

Resistance by government officials in Halifax to provide regular funding for non-Episcopal colleges impeded McCulloch and his mission; however, with the arrival Sir John Sherbrooke as lieutenant-governor in 1811, and for the balance of

His Excellency's five-year term, conditions improved.[279]

The opening quote of this subsection is taken from a tribute that McCulloch gave to Sherbrooke upon his removal to Lower Canada in 1816. The favourable remarks are freely given to a man who could not have been more different than his predecessor. So gratified was McCulloch by the integrity and independence of Sherbrooke that his property, the site of the province's first non-sectarian school of higher learning, was named *Sherbrooke Cottage*.

Chapter 8

WAYFINDING
NAMES

eing *beside* some *thing* of some prominence has always inspired place names. Even a cursory observation of early Mi'kmaw or Acadian place names illustrates this well. It should, then, not be surprising to learn that many house names, like *Cliffside Cottage* in Sydney Mines, or *Parkside* in Truro, also used this effective and accurate formula. Such names are valued for their exact expression and their almost pinpoint identification.

    Kirk is a word used by Scots for "church." *Kirkside*, in Brookfield, Colchester County,[280] could be found near a church, but which one? The Presbyterian Church, of course, as the Kirk is an informal name for the Church of Scotland, a Presbyterian denomination.

    We find *Woodside* in Clifton, Pugwash, Stormont, and Dartmouth; and *Woodside Cottage* in Liscomb and River John. Though pleasing in name, all of these woodside variations are ambiguous given the prevalence of woods. *Sunnyside* sounds like a similarly satisfying situation but offers little aid in orienteering. This popular name appears in Dartmouth, Maitland, Onslow, and Truro. *Sunnyside Cottage* could also be found in Truro and Smiths Cove.

    Brookside beautified Amherst, Halifax, Yarmouth, and Antigonish. *Brookside Cottage* graced Digby, Mount Pleasant, Rogers Hill, and Truro. The latter town also had a variant name, *Burnside*. A *burn* is a Scottish term for "brook."

An illustration of *Brookside*, the Yarmouth residence of N. K. Clements, showing the grounds lavishly laid out after the fashion of English landscape gardening.

Riverside in Bedford and Onslow Station; *Riverside Cottage* in Shubenacadie, Wallace Bridge, Upper Stewiacke, Onslow, and Truro; *River Side Cottage* in Antigonish; *Riverside House* in Murchyville and Lower Truro; and *Riverside Manor* in Bayfield all extol the comforting sights and sounds of gurgling waters and pleasantly situated homes.

An *ingle* is a "hearth." The name *Ingleside*, therefore, creates a most pleasing connotation of warmth—and a warm house is a welcoming one. Isn't it ironic, then, to read of an inhabitant of *Ingleside*, Truro, straying from the Dominion Street residence in 1899? As it turns out, the rambler was just the family's cow.[281] Coincidentally, the same street in Truro accommodated a place named *Marne Hearth*.[282]

As already mentioned, the names of these residences that identified with being beside something often provided some indication of geographic location. Some house names curiously indicated that you weren't quite there yet. *Onaway Cottage* was in Stewiacke,[283] no doubt "on the way" to somewhere else. *Overtheway* in Chester allegedly got its name from the fact that it was "over the way" from the hilltop landmark, Hackmatack Inn.[284] *Moose Path*, near Lake Jolly,[285] was not so much a destination as a starting point for anyone interested in tracking moose.

In like manner, *Lakeside* in Clam Harbour and Lochaber, and *Lakeside Cottage* in Halifax boast enviable surroundings.

Landsdoon perched on a knoll overlooking the town of Truro.

PARKSIDE, LANDSDOON, AND PARK VIEW COTTAGE

Lay thee down upon that rock, my gentle traveler, which the heat of the noon-day sun has warmed, despite the coolness of the neighboring waters—and there, with thy senses half lulled to forgetfulness by the murmurs of the falling stream—thy eyes half closed—and thy spirit all unconscious of earthly turmoils and care—give thyself up to musing, for never was there a more appropriate spot than the Truro Falls.

—Joseph Howe, The *Novascotian*, 1830

The one-time residence of park manager James D. Ross, master of *Landsdoon*, is aptly named,[286] so, too, is *Parkside*, located near the entrance of Truro's Victoria Park.[287] The Ross property is located on a bluff overlooking the Victorian pleasure ground. The backyard drops off sharply into the valley that comprises the beautiful park—*Landsdoon* means "land's end." The street along this brow has adopted the same poetic name though it is now spelled *Lansdoon*. Also on Lansdoon Place was the Dunbar residence named *Park View Cottage*.

Lakeside House, Dartmouth.

LAKESIDE HOUSE

Uriah's tank was almost dry, and after the first squalls had washed the dust from his roof the old man attached the pipes to the gutter, and heard the water go gurgling into his cistern. He listened to the sound, smiling with pleasure; it was grand to get something, even water, for nothing.

—Frank Parker Day, *Rockbound*

Lakeside House at 84 Crichton Avenue in Dartmouth could not be more intimately connected with lake water. Built for John Forbes in 1870, the house overlooks Lake Banook, a site significant for its early associations with the development of hockey. Forbes himself contributed to development of the sport through his invention, the spring skate. Known for his ingenuity, Forbes installed a cistern in the attic of *Lakeside* to collect rainwater and distribute it throughout the house. At the time, the term *lake* was also in use as a reference to "surplus water," as in the description of one Halifax building having "lake water pipes leading to the scullery."[288]

Edgemere House, Dartmouth.

EDGEMERE

Situated across the street from *Lakeside House*, the owners of this property were undaunted by the fact that their neighbour had, as much as thirty-five years earlier, claimed the most appropriate name for this pretty spot overlooking Lake Banook. *Mere*, the suffix in *Edgemere*, means "lake" or "pond," and so the clever residents christened this house with an equivalent though more poetical name.

OCEAN VIEW, SEA SIDE COTTAGE, AND SIMILAR VARIANTS

Sea Side Cottage was at Spencers Island, Cumberland County. The variant *Seaside Cottage* was on the opposite side of the Bay of Fundy both at Centreville, Digby County, and

Ocean View, the Yarmouth residence of Thomas McMurray.

Digby town. With thousands of miles of coastline in this province, many different variations on the "seaside" name must have been devised. *Shore Cottage* in Tatamagouche, *The Breakers* in Pugwash, and *Seahurst* at Spencers Island all conjure up images of warm summer days and bracing ocean air. *Sea View Cottage* (or *Seaview Cottage*) looked out on salt water at Antigonish, Port Caledonia, and Little Bass River. *Seaview* (or *Sea View*) appeared in Dartmouth and South Malagash. *The Rocks* at South Maitland, *The Jib* in Chester, *Ocean View* in Yarmouth, and *Harbor View Cottage* in Pictou Landing all follow the theme.

Bayview (or *Bay View*) documented in Selma, Masstown, Mahone Bay, Musquodoboit Harbour, Smiths Cove, Weymouth, and Central New Annan was the most popular ocean-related name. The *cottage* suffix was added to it for houses in Great Village and Ballentynes Cove. Still other variations were *Bay View House*, Londonderry; *Bay View Villa*, Lower Truro; and *Bay Vue Teras*, Wolfville.

Havenside, Louisbourg, plays on both the nautical and domestic associations of haven.[289] *Haven O'Rest* in Tidnish does likewise, but is there an Irish component to it?

HILLSIDE AND ITS MANY VARIANTS

Amherst, Debert, Middle Stewiacke, Pugwash, Truro, Yarmouth, and Brookfield, Colchester County, were each home to the ubiquitous *Hillside*. The variant *Hillside Cottage* could be found at Acaciaville, Lime Rock, Murchyville, Ballentynes Cove, Deep Brook, Weymouth, and Tatamagouche. *Hillside House*, Truro; *Hillside Lodge*, McCallum Settlement; *Hillside Manor*, Alton; and *Hillside View*, Ecum Secum all looked down on their neighbours. So many *Hillsides* make the name rather tired, if not altogether uninteresting. Switching things up in Salt Springs, Antigonish County, produced *Side Hill Cottage*,[290] but it still comes across as bland. Bayfield had a *Knollside Cottage*.[291] Forest Glen had a *Valley Side Cottage*.[292]

Those possessed of more dash might have derived a similar name using the more poetic *brae*, which is Scottish for "hillside." *The Brae* was a Dartmouth residence. The alliterative *Bonnie Brae* shows up in Smiths Cove, Freeport, and Parrsboro. The equally euphonious *Brae Bonnie* was found in Truro. Frasers Mountain, Pictou County, was home to *Green Brae*.

SPORTSVIEW

The handsome clubhouse of the Truro Amateur Athletic Club (TAAC) was built in 1897. The adjacent track and field facility, said to be a peer to any such grounds in the Maritimes, also accommodated other events, including bicycle races.[293] The clubhouse was built in what was then the western edge of the town amid a rising residential district. Edward F. Wilson, a furniture dealer, had a house here named *Sportsview*,[294] presumably because of its proximity to the TAAC grounds.

Sportsview, Truro (with its Mansard or flat roof), opposite the athletic grounds.

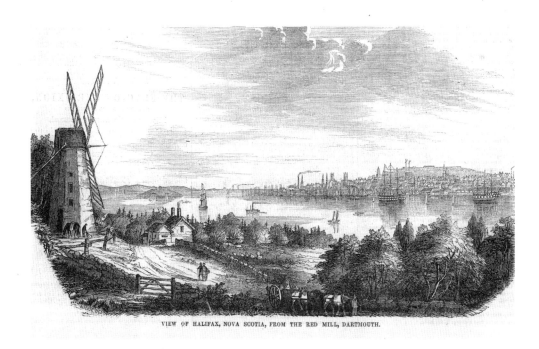

VIEW OF HALIFAX, NOVA SCOTIA, FROM THE RED MILL, DARTMOUTH.

A view of Halifax from the vicinity of *Mill Bank*, Dartmouth.

MILL BANK

The industrial-sounding name *Mill Bank* was fabricated for a Dartmouth residence near Albro Brook, a watercourse that once flowed from Albro Lake to Halifax Harbour. Water power, or water privilege as it was often called, attracted industry to this area just north of downtown Dartmouth. Various types of industry existed along this brook, including Davis's Mill and the Dartmouth Nail Works—both to the immediate east of *Mill Bank*. Further upstream was the rope works of Stairs, Sons & Morrow and the aptly named estate *North Brook*.[295]

The driveway to *Mill Bank* came off of Windmill Road, a significant Dartmouth thoroughfare named for an early windmill that once stood close by and to the northwest of *Mill Bank*. The "red windmill" appears in good order in an 1853 engraving, but by 1901 the ruins were said to have been cleared away. *Mill Bank* was effectively nestled between the red windmill and the water-powered mills of Albro Brook.

ARMDALE

Upon its placid breast—where the blue sky,
And blended rocks, and groves reflected lie.
As round the winding path we onward stroll
Beyond the Isle the Arm's clear waters roll...

—Joseph Howe, "Melville Island"

Halifax's Northwest Arm is an enchanting inlet about three miles long. Its calm expanse is a mecca for watercraft, and its picturesque slopes a refuge from the busyness of life. The rejuvenating powers of the place nourished giants of nation-building: Joseph Howe, Sandford Fleming, and Charles Tupper. The charms of the Northwest Arm loaned much whimsical encouragement to the tradition of house naming, and it is here that a remarkable concentration of names is found, including a number that reference the Arm itself. *Armdale* was the Halifax home of Charles Tupper,[296] and its obvious affection is echoed by *Armbrae,*[297] *Armcroft,*[298] *Armview,*[299] and *Arm Vista.*[300]

LAKELANDS

Lakelands was one of the great country estates of Nova Scotia. In 1857, its boundaries were said to enclose an impressive 700 acres.[301] By 1873, its expanse had absorbed

Lakelands at Lakelands, Hants County.

neighbouring tracts and totalled approximately 3,200 acres with an additional 400 acres in lakes. Truly, the bold name conveyed a credible representation of the place without any fear of overstating the expansive situation. *Lakelands* included two lakes that bordered on what was then called the Windsor Road. The estate included several farms, an inn, a sawmill, and even an Anglican church.[302] The chief homestead consisted of eleven rooms, not counting the workplaces that essentially ran everything: two kitchens, pantries, dairy, cellars, and various outbuildings. A second house contained nine rooms exclusive of its own similar network of ancillary rooms. The lakes were said to abound with trout and contain two good sites for mills.[303]

Chapter 9

NAMES *to* IMPRESS

It may be that no better vehicle for dropping names has ever been devised. House naming unabashedly, perhaps even righteously, engages in this all-too-human and ever-tempting pretension. Of course, it had to happen. The tradition of house naming, with its ennobling quality and promulgating nature had, and has, an attraction for ambitious and socially mobile people. From royal or famous acquaintances to ignoble allusions of well-placed ancestors, this category of house naming is rich and intriguing. This chapter identifies a number of property names that possess that quality of cultivating approbation. House names of this type were generally expressive of some moment in time when one had the occasion to have brushed with someone famous or to have served under a noble officer. As noted in a previous chapter, it may be a well-placed ancestor that provides the opportunity for name dropping. A house name of this type could accentuate a flimsy connection with an important person or simply serve as a nod to their honour and respectability.

MOUNT EDWARD

That, Mr. Slick, contains all the Prince's correspondence with my father and all the letters of his to others that could be collected; also His Royal Highness's orderly books, thirteen of them; and also my poor father's journal while the Prince was here.

—T. C. Haliburton, *Sam Slick's Wise Saws and Modern Instances,* 1853

Prince Edward Augustus, Duke of Kent and Strathearn.

Mount Edward, built by William Burch Brinley, was located on the old Preston Road, Dartmouth. It was named in honour of Prince Edward, Duke of Kent and Strathearn, who was stationed in Halifax from 1794 to 1800.[304] The family had a connection to Prince Edward and what better way to remind folks of the fact than to dedicate their home to the much-loved duke. William's father, George, had been deputy commissary-general at Halifax in 1797 and afterwards elevated to commissary-general until his death in 1809. William's mother was a sister to Lady Francis Wentworth. The latter, with husband Sir John Wentworth loaned their estate to Prince Edward for the duration of his command at Halifax.

KENT LODGE

HRH Edward, Duke of Kent and Strathearn, was commander of British forces in Nova Scotia while stationed at Halifax. In June of 1794, Edward travelled on horseback from Halifax to Annapolis Royal, stopping in Wolfville where the leading man of the village, Judge Elisha DeWolf, accommodated and entertained the prince in his hospitable cottage.[305] As a means of recalling the honour of hosting such a distinguished guest, DeWolf's house was named *Kent Lodge*. Similarly, Horton Corner, just seven miles

Kent Lodge, Wolfville.

west, was renamed Kentville. The *lodge* suffix is noteworthy in that it attempts to down-play or soften the Duke of Kent association, almost as if to say offhandedly, "Yeah, the Duke of Kent stayed here—it's no big deal," with a wink and a nod.

MOUNT RUNDELL AND YORK LODGE

Mount Rundell, once likened to a well-kept English country house—"a charming place, quite English"—was built by mining engineer Richard Smith shortly after his 1827 arrival in Nova Scotia. Smith had been hand-picked by the General Mining Association (GMA) of London to develop the coal and iron industry of the colony. The GMA had obtained mineral leases from Prince Frederick, Duke of York, who in 1826 had been granted all of the then ungranted mineral lands of Nova Scotia, ostensibly to help him deal with the clamour of creditors—much of his insolvent state resulted

Mount Rundell, Stellarton.

from an affinity for gambling.[306] Two of the duke's creditors were John Bridge and Philip Rundell, business partners who had made their mark as prominent gold- and silversmiths and whose interests also extended to other minerals. The GMA was a Rundell subsidiary, and so it was Rundell's name that Smith attached to the place.[307]

The seventy-five-acre estate was laid out in the English style with a sweeping carriage drive, massive sandstone gateposts, a gatehouse, coach house, barns, hot houses, tennis courts, gardens, orchard, and pigeon cote. The estate staff were housed in cottages on-site and were predominantly former black slaves who had been liberated from southern plantations during the War of 1812.[308]

Mount Rundell, with its massive fifty-by-two-hundred-foot footprint, was built to impress and entertain visitors of high positions. It could not handle all the traffic, so another house was built nearby. The second residence was named *York Lodge* in honour of the financially challenged duke.[309]

Mount Rundell is not connected with the later-named, alternately spelled, Mount Rundle, which looms over Banff, Alberta.

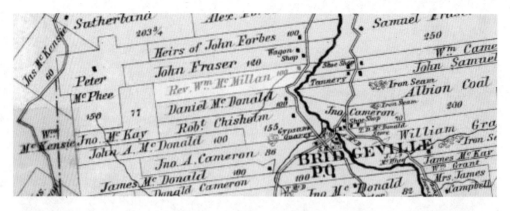

Dufferin Cottage, the property of Rev. William McMillan, from the *Illustrated Historical Atlas of Pictou County*, 1879.

DUFFERIN COTTAGE

In July 1873, Lord Dufferin, Governor General of Canada, sailed into Pictou Harbour as part of a Maritime tour to familiarize himself with the nascent country of which he was queen's representative. The visit to Pictou was brief, and it appears the chief object of it was the coal mines. Both Lord and Lady Dufferin went ashore, where more than half the inhabitants assembled at the landing to greet Their Excellencies. Emblems, banners, streamers, and flowers welcomed the visitors as they made their way to Albion Mines (Stellarton).

Once there, Lord and Lady Dufferin observed the surface workings, but his Lordship was keen to see more. Surprising his hosts, he donned a miner's wardrobe and descended the shaft with mine officials. Once at the underground coal face, he obtained a pick from one of the miners and worked for half an hour to the delight of the stalwart colliers.[310] The principal ventilator for the shaft was named the "Lady Dufferin" and the two engines that ran it were named the "Lord Dufferin" and the "Lady Victoria."[311] Streets and place names within the county similarly recall that memorable day when a lord and lady endeared themselves to citizens. *Dufferin Cottage*, in Bridgeville,[312] is also believed to have derived its name from that wellspring of sentiment connected to July 24, 1873.

FROGMORE

Of partridge wings in secret thickets gray,
The marriage hymns of all the birds at play,
The faces of sweet flowers, and easeful dreams
Beside slow reaches of frog-haunted streams

—Archibald Lampman, "April" from *Lyrics of Earth, Sonnets and Ballads*, 1925

You might wonder how an estate with a peculiar name like *Frogmore* hopes to convey a sense of respect and good taste when its name conjures up associations with slimy amphibious creatures, who unless they happen to be transformed princes, are likely unaccustomed to the refinements of society. The funny thing about this Aylesford home is that its name actually does have a connection to royalty. *Frogmore*, you see, is also the name of one of the residences of the British royal family. It was a favourite retreat of Queen Victoria and the place where she and Prince Albert are buried.[313]

The origins of how Aylesford's *Frogmore* got its name are uncertain; however, it is noteworthy that its owner, Henry Van Buskirk (c. 1767–1841), came to Nova Scotia as a Loyalist. His father, Lawrence Van Buskirk, was a captain in the King's Orange Rangers and brought the family to Saint John in 1783. Shortly after, they left New Brunswick for Kentville, and finally settled down at Aylesford. It is likely that a proud military heritage, characterized by loyalty to the king, provided the impetus for selecting a house name borrowed from a royal residence. It is interesting that Fredericton, New Brunswick, also has its own *Frogmore* with its motivations pointing toward the royal residence.

WALTON COTTAGE

Beginning in 1847, Andrew Downs (1811–1892) established a zoological gardens just outside Halifax on the Northwest Arm at a place he called *Walton Cottage*. The site grew from an original five acres to one hundred acres as the naturalist expanded his collection and developed his grounds.[314] As the earliest zoological gardens on the American continent,[315] the site came to enjoy renown as interest in the subject of natural history experienced tremendous advancement at this time. In England, naturalist Charles Waterton (1782–1865), had earlier established the world's first wildfowl and nature reserve at his home, *Walton Hall*.[316]

Downs actually visited the famed Waterton in 1864, during one of several trips he made to Europe. In "Reminiscences of Andrew Downs," his friend and fellow

The zoological gardens known as Downs's Aviary was opened by Andrew Downs of *Walton Cottage*, Halifax.

naturalist, Major General Campbell Hardy wrote that Downs named his home *Walton Cottage* after visiting Waterton at *Walton Hall*. Reportedly not fond of letter writing, Downs prized his correspondence with Waterton, calling him, "My worthy master in ornithology."[317]

Rainham also known as *Thornleigh*, Wolfville.

RAINHAM

Sir Charles James Townshend (1844–1924) rose through legal and political ranks to become the twelfth chief justice of Nova Scotia. He claimed to be descended from the noble Townshends of Norfolk,[318] a family that produced a number of chief justices. Biographer Philip Girard notes the family connection is shrouded in doubt. Whether fact or fiction, the assertion prompted Sir Charles to name his summer residence in Wolfville *Rainham*,[319] after the splendid seat of the Townshend family in Norfolk, which was built in the seventeenth century and named *Raynham Hall*.

Chapter 10

MILITARY HONOURS

War is a brutal thing. It should not be celebrated. At the same time, war often goes hand in hand with acts of bravery, selfless giving, and freedom from tyranny. Elements such as these should be revered. Duty, honour, and service with distinction are similarly worthy of pride and respect. It is these positive aspects of what is an otherwise violent and senseless business that compel communities to erect memorial cenotaphs and commemorative monuments. In the same way, the naming or renaming of towns, ships, homes, and other objects have always served as ways of expressing regard for valour, victory, and victim.

House names of this type are certainly uncommon; moreover, they can be difficult to identify so many years later, as evidenced by a place called *Kimberley*. A pleasant-sounding house name like *Kimberley*, noted later in this chapter, would not normally produce any intimation of a connection with a military engagement, but its context of time and place almost require a military interpretation.

LADYSMITH

Hence, despots join to end thy sway,
And substitute their tyrant reign;
But bravely still hold on thy way,
And still for freedom rule the main.

—James D. Ross, "The Diamond Jubilee Rule Britannia," 1897
lyrics in *Truro Daily News*, October 26, 1899

The Boer War (1899–1902) served to heighten already-strong sentiment for the British Empire in much of English-speaking Canada. This admiration for the empire and the overwhelming sense that it was a righteous power providing justice and security throughout the world inspired Nova Scotians to service and allegiance.

Even today, the Boers' 118-day siege of Ladysmith makes for absolutely gripping reading. News reports were received daily by telegraph cable—the first time Nova Scotians had experienced such compelling and up-to-date detail of a war in which their own sons and daughters (nurses) were engaged. The troops in Ladysmith—on rations, under constant siege, and with escape cut off—put up a valiant but tenuous

Ladysmith, Truro, circled on an 1878 map of the town.

resistance to the Boers day after day. It was a real-life serial that served to whip citizens up into a "Rule Britannia" type of fervour. News of Nova Scotians killed or wounded touched everyone. Truro even had its own war correspondent in the person of W. E. Trueman, a *Truro Daily News* staffer who enlisted to fight at the first opportunity.[320]

After British troops finally managed to relieve the garrison, a Park Street residence in Truro commemorated the heroic defence by being named *Ladysmith*.[321] This was the home of Sarah V. Mack. Her maiden name was Smith, and so the name cleverly possesses a dual meaning.

SPION KOP AND KIMBERLEY

Spion Kop was the site of another battle during the Boer War. *Spion* means "spy" or "look-out" and *kop* means "hill." Taking the kop and thereby occupying a commanding position was the goal of this British assault in January 1900. D. J. Thomas's house in Truro shared somewhat similar topography situated on a steep terrace, overlooking the town, and he named his residence *Spion Kop*. Choosing such a name, though the motivation is unfortunately unconfirmed, is highly suggestive of a connection with, or inspiration derived from, the South African campaign.

In the same way, the Truro property *Kimberley* (not shown), is likely named for the

Spion Kop, Truro.

Siege of Kimberley, a British victory during the Boer War, and one that took place just months before a building contractor turned the sod to begin construction of the fine residence designed by Truro architect Dougald Henderson.[322] It would be difficult to imagine someone choosing a name like *Kimberley* at such a time if there was no intention to have people draw a direct connection to the South African battle. It is worthwhile to consider the motivations behind *Ladysmith*, *Spion Kop*, and *Kimberley*. To have three residences in a single Nova Scotia town honour three recent battles of the British Empire makes a significant statement about how common citizens regarded patriotism and the role of Britain in the world at that time.

AZIMGHUR

Azimghur Cottage,[323] or simply *Azimghur* as it was also known, was located on Halifax's Northwest Arm near Melville Cove. The residence was built by a Sergeant Macnamara, who served with British forces and Ghurka allies in the Indian Mutiny of 1857.[324] *Azimghur Cottage* glorified the triumphant struggle for the town of Azimghur, in central India, when rebellious sepoys roamed the region at will. In July of 1857, sepoys attacked Azimghur with a force reported to be ten times as large as the garrison in the town. With under three hundred men and a single old cannon fit for nothing more

Azimghur Cottage, Northwest Arm, Halifax.

than noon-day salutes, Deputy Magistrate Edward F. Venables ordered a new gun carriage and grapeshot be made. The mutinous sepoys attempted charge after charge, each one coming within one hundred yards before being driven back by the grapeshot. After heavy losses, the assailants lost heart.[325] Several other conflicts throughout 1857 and 1858 saw Azimghur regularly threatened.

GRENADIER FORT

Grenadier Fort, Halifax.

Hastily built wooden fortifications were thrown up along the perimeter of the fledgling settlement of Halifax in its first few years. One of these was Grenadier Fort, which included a blockhouse and occupied ground in the vicinity of Jacob Street. But what was defined as the perimeter of the nascent town was quickly overtaken by the needs of an expanding population. A barracks existed here as early as 1769,[326] and its usefulness no doubt outlasted the blockhouse, though it too was eventually disposed of by military officials. The barracks found new purpose as a residence for Captain Thomas Maynard, RN, and continued to bear its historic name *Grenadier Fort.* Historic records show the residence was still known as *Grenadier Fort* when listed for sale in 1857 to settle the estate of the recently deceased captain.[327]

FORT MASSEY

The defences of early Halifax consisted of more than one dozen strategic points, all garrisoned and developed in relation to their military importance. One of these defences was a redoubt at a place called Fort Massey, a blockhouse and barracks on an elevated position in the present-day vicinity of South and Queen Streets. This site was developed under the command of Lieutenant General Eyre Massey in 1776,[328] and takes its name from Massey, who was commanding officer in Nova Scotia from 1776 to 1778.[329] The military value of this site quickly waned and the fort fell into disrepair. Names have a way of lingering, though, and by 1858 with no trace of the old fort, the area still referred to as Fort Massey was carved into building lots[330] and a soldiers' cemetery.[331] One of the more impressive residences in this growing part of the peninsula was the home of William Blowers Bliss (1795–1874), a well-connected citizen of high character, and an esteemed barrister and judge.

Period references to Bliss's residence call it *Fort Massey*,[332] though it is not known whether the judge enthusiastically embraced the name or merely surrendered to what was already a well-entrenched association with his grounds and the neighbourhood.

ALMA VILLA

Bright o'er the ripp'ling Alma,
The autumn sunbeams shone
On martial hosts—on glittering steel,
And battlements of stone

—Charles Fenerty, "Battle of the Alma," 1854

It was the fall of 1854, and many of the world's great powers were at war. The Crimean War had officially been under way for a year with Turkey and Russia the chief combatants, while Britain and France strategized and mobilized. Bits of five-week-old news reached Halifax intermittently that first year, and then the big news poured in: a great victory involving tens of thousands at Alma!

Exultation and pride filled the newspapers. It was a brilliant achievement—a victory for a just cause—and something more, as a Halifax newspaper proclaimed, "For the first time in history the soldiers of England and France have trod the bloody track of victory side by side, and mingled the banners of the two Empires in one trophy."[333]

A fervid ripple emanated throughout the world with that victory at Alma. Ships, towns, babies, halls, and houses were christened with the honoured name. Adam Reid, a long-standing member of the militia unit known as the 3rd Halifax Rifles and by 1856 lieutenant colonel of that unit,[334] was naturally disposed to some expression of his own regarding the triumph. Naming his residence *Alma Villa* was his authentic response.

As an additional layer of meaning, *Alma Villa* overlooked the rifle range at

Alma Villa, Bedford, 1958.

Bedford. Reid's son-in-law, Major John Corbin, helped establish the facility in the 1860s in an effort to improve marksmanship.[335]

Chapter 11

REST *and*
RELAXATION

❧

The names of some properties, many of which were likely summer retreats, tend to reflect an easygoing sentiment. These properties are more likely than any other type to express a sort of proclamation of how to live, and they do this with a name. *Haven O' Rest* and *Kamp Kumfort* were a couple of summer homes in the Tidnish area.[336] Hunting is some folks' idea of a leisurely pursuit, and so *Gunner's Retreat*,[337] also in Tidnish, and *Moose Path*[338] near Lake Jolly are suggestive of a sportsman's paradise.

This chapter ends with two properties that have bungalow-inspired names. The bungalow was not just an architectural style but also it was a sort of marriage between architecture and easy living. The bungalow was a phenomenon that epitomizes the sentiment that the house names of this chapter attempt to convey, and for that reason, it poses an ideal place to end.

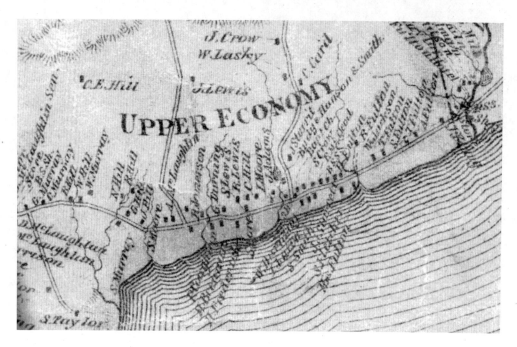

Upper Economy shore, where *Bide-a-wee Cottage* was located.

BIDE-A-WEE COTTAGE

Is the road very dreary?
Patience yet!
Rest will be sweet if thou art weary,
And after night cometh the morning cheery.
Then bide a wee, and dinna fret.

—Author Unknown, *Colchester Sun*, October 31, 1877

The only knowledge of *Bide-a-wee Cottage* in Upper Economy is a snippet of news that intimated a Colchester lady and her two Boston nieces were to spend a few weeks there in the summer of 1906, bathing and enjoying the scenery. The party's blithe and carefree ambition seems to affirm the name of their intended haven which means "stay awhile." *Bide-a-wee Cottage* was one of many similarly named properties that conveyed a definite sense of Shangri-La—an escape from the busyness of life. It is almost as if such a name had a power to proclaim, "Toil and trouble have no authority in this place."

Belleville, Pictou, 1879.

BELLEVILLE

Belleville was the Pictou home of James Fogo, JP. Though the named property can be traced back to an 1850 reference under the ownership of Hugh Denoon,[339] James Fogo is reported to have built his house there in 1854, perhaps replacing an earlier one. Fogo's Tuscany-style villa with beautiful surroundings suited the home's "beautiful villa" namesake. The property's 180 acres were contained just within the eastern edge of the town limits, and the villa was situated to afford a commanding view of the surrounding country. A summer scene was said to present an exceedingly pleasing panorama of animated character with vessels of all descriptions plying to and fro upon the waters. The property comprised one of Pictou County's notable and valuable freestone quarries supplying thousands of tons of building stone to many projects, including bridges for the Intercolonial Railway.[340]

SAINT'S REST

Saint's Rest, Bass River.

Not far from the Economy shore, the Bass River empties into the Bay of Fundy. It is here that *Saint's Rest*, the home of D. S. Collins, could be found. In the early 1900s, it could boast of having all the modern household conveniences: garden plot, stable, carriage house, and even an ice house.[341] During the summer, the veranda was an outdoor parlour, bathed in sunlight and congested with grass mats, hammock, and gramophone. Before long, others wanted a share in this salubrious situation and built their own retreats. The shoreline itself became synonymous with the Collins's cottage and the area assumed the *Saint's Rest* name, which it carries to this day.

ATLASMOOK

With mute amaze,
And earnest gaze,
Seated round his cot
Entranced, and to the spot
Enchained, we listen to the story,
Catching glimpses of the glory...

—Silas T. Rand, "The Dying Indian's Dream," 1858

The Rev. J. M. Fisher had a house of some renown. The Hantsport residence was celebrated for its delightful specimens of antiquarian lore and works of genius.[342] Now, whether this was just a fancy reference to antiques and old books is not known, but the interesting reverend seemed just the sort to adopt a house name that would provoke curiosity. *Atlasmook*,[343] a name of Mi'kmaw nomenclature, means "to repose." An alternate spelling of the residence has also been found, *Atlasmooak*, and it similarly means "to rest."[344]

Reverend Fisher likely selected a Mi'kmaw name not just as a nod to the Mi'kmaq but also to fellow Hantsport minister Silas T. Rand, who established a Mi'kmaw mission there. It was Rand who had translated the Bible into Mi'kmaw and who, in 1888, compiled the Mi'kmaw-English Dictionary, which Reverend Fisher may have perused to select a house name. Like Fisher, Rand collected antiquarian objects, the latter reverend having a particular interest in items of Mi'kmaw origin.[345]

AIRY PLACE

Airy was at one time a highly estimable attribute used to describe a home or schoolhouse or any other building that one would expect to inhabit for hours at a time. *Airy* of course means "abounding in fresh air." In terms of local historic architecture, the word

Airy Place was located under the treed canopy of Elm Street, Truro.

carried a strong connotation of healthfulness. Conversely, constricted or stale places were believed to encourage such early scourges as cholera, diphtheria, and scarlet fever. Surprisingly, air flow was an early consideration in the construction and layout of many of our region's houses.[346] *Airy Place* in Truro[347] was, therefore, a residence that laid claim to promoting a healthful constitution.

It should also be pointed out that Airy (alternately Erie, Urie, etc.) is a surname of British origin. It is not known if that surname has any connection to the family heritage of former residents of *Airy Place*.

KOZYHOLME KOTTAGE

Kozyholme Kottage, located at Onslow Station, Colchester County, was the comfortable home of Jennie Wilson's uncle, Peter Hall. Jennie found the place so cozy that she was married there in 1919.

SANS SOUCI

This Chester property bears a French language name. *Sans* means "without," and *souci* means "worry." The name translates as "carefree." *Sans Souci* was the summer home of a Baltimore doctor named Charles E. Simon, who with his family, visited Chester

Sans Souci, Chester.

every summer for rest and recuperation. Dr. Simon is said to have been one of the earliest and most devoted summer residents of Chester.[348] The name may have been popularized by Prussian king Frederick the Great, whose summer palace at Potsdam was named *Sanssouci*.

BELLEVUE

And ever see the blinded lying low
At Bellevue, Camp Hill, and College Hall;
And ever see the corpses, row on row,
Their mangled faces covered with a pall

—D. M. Matheson, "December Sixth, 1917"

It seems any residence bearing the name *Bellevue* is invariably true to its namesake and possessed of a "beautiful view" and often situated in a commanding position. The relatively common name appears twice in Halifax, with *Bellevue* on Gottingen Street and *Bellevue House*[349] on Spring Garden Road. The "beautiful view" can often go the other way, too, as passersby travelling Gottingen Street on one particular day in 1860

Bellevue House, Spring Garden Road, Halifax.

would have taken notice of Hon. W. A. Black's *Bellevue* with pretty trees surrounding it, all illuminated with coloured lights and a fountain "in full play" on the lawn in front.[350] This illumination though was not an everyday practice; the occasion was the royal visit of HRH the Prince of Wales.

BELVEDERE

Much of South End Halifax was a rural setting of fields and fences, apart from Point Pleasant, when John Bazalgette lived at *Belvedere*, near the intersection of Tower Road and Inglis Street. Bazalgette sold the property in 1857 when a real estate advertising poster lauded the property as "one of the most eligible and delightful residences on the peninsula." The listing further noted *Belvedere*'s situation: commanding a fine view of the Citadel, harbour, and surrounding country.[351] It was the cleared land and resultant views that made *Belvedere*'s name so appropriate. The word *belvedere* is derived from Italian origins. The Italian word *bel* or *bello*, meaning "beautiful" and the verb *vedere*, meaning "to see or view," combine to give us *belvedere*.

A painting by Alexander Cavalié Mercer, c. 1841, illustrating the view from *Belvedere*.

BROOK HOUSE

You think you have reached the limit of the town, but go a step further and you will find that some mortal happier than all the rest has his quiet home away at the "back of beyond," seeking and enjoying peaceful mornings and evenings with wife and weans.

—A description of Dartmouth from *Presbyterian Witness*, September 6, 1879

This residence with the rural-sounding name was indeed a country residence situated in a picturesque neighbourhood about two miles from the Dartmouth ferry. It contained about fifty acres of land and presumably took its name from the brook that ran through it, acknowledged in an 1851 real estate advertisement as "a constant stream of water."[352] The grounds contained walks cut through the woods, fruit trees, and a fish pond near the house.[353] The dwelling itself had six bedrooms with suites for servants.

UNADILLA

Unadilla sounds more like the name of some prehistoric animal or a mythical beast than a house; however, the name of this Jollimore residence once owned by A. E. McManus was said to mean "house of peace." The name was supposedly picked up as a "souvenir" from a trip to the Patagonia region of South America by a son of Mr. McManus.[354] *Unadilla* can also be found as a place name in several American states, where sources there claim an Iroquoian origin, meaning "pleasant valley" or "pleasant region."[355]

Unadilla, Jollimore, Halifax.

LAWN COTTAGE

What might seem like a thoroughly pedestrian name has to be put in context to fully appreciate its meaning. The name *Lawn Cottage* comes from Dartmouth in 1885.[356] When the name came into use and when it vanished is not known; all that exists is merely a single reference gleaned from a wedding announcement. The time, though, was an important one for the development of that urban obsession of trying to make two blades of grass grow where but one grew before. The advancement of lawn games provided additional impetus in the quest for a green carpet, with tennis, croquet, and quoits being popular pursuits.[357]

Lawn mowers by this time were of the simple mechanical variety that operated with revolving knives in a cylindrical housing and were powered by the forward movement of the operator. The machines weighed about forty pounds and cut a ten-inch swath.[358] Lawn sprinklers and garden hoses were also available at this early date,[359] although the old-fashioned scythe continued to trim lawns into the twentieth century.[360]

While nothing regarding Dartmouth's *Lawn Cottage* is definitively known, the name enjoyed widespread use in Britain and originated from an ever-growing appreciation for the landscape aesthetic.

WINDLEBLOW

Tell me, ye winged winds,
That round my pathway roar,
Do you know some spot
Where mortals weep no more!

—*Yarmouth Herald*, March 6, 1856

Windleblow of Folly Lake is essentially a whimsical spelling for "wind will blow." It is a cheerfully optimistic name for a summer retreat equipped with a boathouse and boats.[361] The name *Windleblow* encompasses something more though: a *windle* is a part of a fishing rod, a winch or a reel. This clever name therefore incorporates a number of positive summer associations, including mosquito-free breezes, sailing, and fishing.

Wyndrift[362] and *Windyholme*,[363] both of Bible Hill, also indicate a fondness for breezes as does Wolfville's *Windmere Cottage*.[364] The word *windmere* loosely translates to the less poetic "sea breeze."

An unidentified cottage on Folly Lake in Colchester County, 1915.

THE BUNGALOW

A million men to settle down
Near as they can to Digby town
Healthy, strong, both wise and witty,
The kind we want to build a city.

—H. C. G., *Digby Weekly Courier*, August 14, 1903

The bungalow was an early twentieth-century house style that really gained "feverish appeal" by 1910,[365] and continued its popularity throughout that decade and into the twenties. The bungalow's philosophy dovetailed with that of the Arts and Crafts Movement, an inescapable influence of the period and a movement to which the bungalow owes its aesthetic.

The Bungalow, Queen Street, Digby.

Before the bungalow became an international trend, and even before the concept of it became fully articulated, there was *The Bungalow*. In 1899, Digby's first bungalow was being constructed and by March of 1900, the *Digby Weekly Courier* was offered a tour of the modish domicile. The press declared, "The house contains every convenience pertaining to a first-class residence."[366] Owner H. Crosskill definitively dubbed the new innovation *The Bungalow* as if it were the only one. Well, it sort of was the only one. There were no other bungalows in Digby at the time; indeed, it would be ten years or more before some Nova Scotian towns built their first bungalow.[367]

The bungalow was a departure in home design. Here was a house style that sanctioned single-storey living in the name of convenience. The fully articulated expression of the style emphasized simple comfort in a modest-sized dwelling; however, early examples of the style, like Crosskill's, were actually quite commodious. *The Bungalow* boasted a drawing room, dining room, kitchen, pantry, three bedrooms, trunk room, bathroom, and coat closet all on one floor.[368] A veranda extended living space to the outdoors.[369] The foundation was of concrete—a novelty at this time.

SUMMER RESIDENCE OF HENRY
ROPER ON THE EASTERN SIDE
OF THE NORTHWEST ARM.

"IDEAL" BUNGALOW AND BOATHOUSE AT
MARLBOROUGH WOODS.

A type of many pretty and comfortable private summer homes at the far-famed Northwest Arm.

The Ideal Bungalow, Northwest Arm, Halifax.

THE IDEAL BUNGALOW

Before the First World War, a land development syndicate calling itself the Northwest Arm Land Company purchased much of the former *Belmont* estate in Halifax's South End. Grand plans for the subdivision contained parklands, public walkways, winding avenues, and public access to the Northwest Arm. Despite the attractiveness of the plans, with its *City Beautiful* influence, buyers were not lining up. As the scheme struggled, some shareholders bought out their shares, but the principals, including Vice-President Henry Roper, held steadfast. In 1907, the land company redoubled its efforts with a renewed advertising campaign and subdivision plan, which featured the park in a prominent fashion. The boldfaced caption below the illustration read, "An ideal summer spot for your summer bungalow." With a direct connection to the ad, Henry Roper's home, *The Ideal Bungalow*, located adjacent to the park, was opened for viewing to help entice potential buyers. Still, sales were slow and the First World War did nothing to improve prospects. By the early 1920s, the North West Arm Land Company was defunct. It would be another two decades before the market was ready to embrace the subdivision.[370]

CONCLUSION

❦

This in-depth look at some of Nova Scotia's named residences endeavours to showcase sites from across the entire province. This has not been without some challenges; chief among them is the uneven distribution of surviving names. Two locales stand out as possessing a rich inventory of names, and as a result, these places figure prominently, if not somewhat disproportionately, in this book. Of the 1,000 names identified during research for this book, 58 come from the Northwest Arm area of Halifax and a staggering 142 come from the community of Truro–Bible Hill. So, one in five names come from these two small geographic areas. Would it be historically accurate to declare that 20 percent of Nova Scotia's named houses could be found in these two locales? Not likely.

One reason so many of the Northwest Arm names have survived is that much has been written about these homes and their inhabitants. Indeed, the latter is most compelling. In 1908, John Regan wrote in *Sketches and Traditions of the Northwest Arm*, "A glimpse at the annals of the Northwest Arm is almost equal to a peep into a hall of fame—scientists, soldiers, statesmen, poets, orators, prelates, admirals, generals, captains of industry and kings of finance" called this place home. Joseph Howe, Charles Tupper, Sandford Fleming, of course these giants of our history and scores of others and their accomplishments—and their homes—are recorded for posterity. It may have been that owning a home in the company of prominent people and in close proximity to such enchanting scenery, as is featured in abundance on the Arm, assisted somewhat in creating the conditions that encouraged house naming. Here were all the picturesque prerequisites and trappings of patricians—natural inspiration hand in hand with high society. It is unsurprising that house names would thrive, even become a part of the culture of the area, and survive to the present.

What of Truro–Bible Hill? Was this a hive of house naming, or like the Northwest Arm is there some means of explaining how so many of the community's names found their way into the printed word and thereby secured their immortality? It seems the answer lies with the *Truro Daily News* and its esteemed editor, Wilbert D. Dimock. Truro was a town of a size that was right in the "sweet spot": large enough for an eight-page daily newspaper but not too large to do away with nosy tidbits that dealt with the comings and goings of ordinary citizens. Most critical of all is that the town had an editor who appeared to possess an affinity for house names. W. D. Dimock lived at *Forest Lawn*. His sister Alice lived at nearby *Scrivelsby*. This news brief from 1907 was attributed to him and is classic Dimock fare: "As Dr. Kinsman and Mr. Albert Harty were walking on Prince St., West at noon today, a handsome deer, disturbed doubtless by that gamy cocker-spaniel, 'Screech-Owl,' came bounding through the garden at 'Forest Lawn,' leaped the fence into the street, rushed across into neighboring property, took the fence in the rear of 'Stonycroft' and made with the fleetness of the wind in the direction of the new golf club house; in a rush likely to get there in time for the house-warming on Victoria Day evening."[371]

Dimock's newspaper clearly mentions house names with a frequency that far exceeds that of any other newspaper in the province. The paper presents a bounteous source of house names, not just for Truro, but for much of the province as community correspondents from many counties regularly submitted "newsy notes" detailing the happenings in their home communities. In fact, of the 1,000 house names identified in research for this book, 431 appear in the *Truro Daily News* at least once—of course the local names appeared with regularity, particularly Dimock's own *Forest Lawn*—perhaps his favourite subject next to his cocker-spaniel, "Screech-Owl."

This time capsule of Truro names left to us by Dimock[372] permits us, to some degree, to extrapolate the house-naming tradition over the rest of the province. Given that Truro boasted a minimum of 142 house names in the early twentieth century, a simple comparison to other communities allows one to scale up or down as required to estimate how pervasive the practice might have been across the province. Furthermore, it can be expected that Dimock was likely not exhaustive in his knowledge of Truro names, that many names would have been of a lesser known, even more private variety, and that many people would not have had the occasion or inclination to be noticed by the local news. These preceding factors would suggest that the number of 142 may be accepted as low—how low is impossible to state—but the Truro precinct clearly illustrates the tradition of house naming was far more ubiquitous than what we generally tend to believe and far more middle class than what is suggested by the grand estate names that we learn of in biographies of accomplished men and women.

One final thought on this fine tradition of house naming is that we should not permit it to fade away. The custom has been in decline for many decades, but like a coat of paint or a neatly mown lawn it contributes to the aesthetics and pride of our residences. It also has value as a part of our culture, and while its historic practice and subsequent decline are not exclusive to Nova Scotia, a renewed interest in it can contribute to maintaining a sense of place and a unique way of life that marks Nova Scotia and Bluenose culture as distinct. Perhaps this book will serve as a small encouragement to revive this custom. Consider a name for your own property, and remember that house naming doesn't have to be pretentious, but it does give one permission to be pretentious.

ENDNOTES

INTRODUCTION

1. *Truro Daily News*, July 5, 1906, 4.

2. Annie B. Fairbanks, *The Journals of Hon. John Eleazer Fairbanks from 1816 to 1855*, Nova Scotia Archives Library, request slip G 475 F35 1998, 225–227.

3. *McAlpine's Halifax City Directory for 1872–73* (Halifax: David McAlpine), 17.

4. *Colchester Sun*, March 13, 1889.

5. *Truro Daily News*, June 18, 1909, 5.

6. *Digby Weekly Courier*, July 27, 1900, 3.

7. *Truro Daily News*, April 5, 1905, 7.

8. *Halifax Herald*, June 4, 1908, 7.

9. A. J. Downing, *Landscape Gardening and Rural Architecture* (New York: Dover Publications, 1991), 320.

10. *Truro Daily News*, May 9, 1893, 1.

11. *Yarmouth Herald*, February 13, 1873, 4.

12. *The Gazetteer and Guide to the Maritime Provinces for 1876-77* (Halifax: Charles D. McAlpine, 1876), 85.

CHAPTER 1

13. *Presbyterian Witness*, September 6, 1879, 284.

14. *Truro Daily News*, May 4, 1901, 3.

15. *Truro Daily News*, May 1, 1905, 5.

16. *Truro Daily News*, May 19, 1897, 4.

17. *Truro Daily News*, March 18, 1904, 4.

18. John W. Regan, *Sketches and Traditions of the Northwest Arm* (Halifax: McAlpine Publishing, 1908), 140.

19. Philip Woodfine and Claire Gapper, "Stanyan, Abraham (1672–1732)," in *Oxford Dictionary of National Biography* (Oxford: Oxford University Press, 2004).

20. Arthur Wentworth Hamilton Eaton, *Chapters in the History of Halifax, Nova Scotia* (n.p., 1915), 279.

21. Richard P. Hallowell, "The Pioneer Quakers" (Boston: Houghton Mifflin, 1887), 70.

22. Phyllis R. Blakeley, "Piers, Temple Foster," in *Dictionary of Canadian Biography*, vol. 8, University of Toronto/ Université Laval, 2003–, accessed June 1, 2016, http://www.biographi.ca/en/ bio/piers_temple_foster_8E.html.

23. Janet Kitz, *Andrew Cobb Architect and Artist* (Halifax: Nimbus Publishing, 2014), 44.

24. *Colchester Sun*, June 4, 1890.

25. *Colchester Sun*, September 5, 1877.

26. *Truro Daily News* October 22, 1891, 1.

27. James D. Cameron, *For the People: A History of St. Francis University* (Montreal: McGill-Queen's University Press, 1996), 140.

28. *Truro Daily News*, August 21, 1907, 7.

29. Rev. Dr. Moses M. Coady, *Masters of Their Own Destiny* (n.p., 1939), 6.

30. *Royal Gazette and the Nova-Scotia Advertiser*, May 18, 1790, 2.

CHAPTER 2

31. Regan, *Sketches and Traditions of the Northwest Arm*, 61.

32. Regan, *Sketches and Traditions of the Northwest Arm*, 65.

33. *Truro Daily News*, July 11, 1899, 3.

34. RootsWeb.com, Ancestry.com, updated 2017-10-04 05:31:02, accessed June 25, 2018, https://wc.rootsweb.ancestry.com/cgi-bin/igm.cgi?op=GET&db=-bonniekgorman&id=I45&style=TEXT.

35. Eldon Hay, *Chignecto Covenanters* (Montreal: McGill-Queens University Press, 1996), 39.

36. Henry J. Morgan, ed., *The Canadian Parliamentary Companion* (Montreal[?]: n.p., 1872), 388.

37. Grant Allan Lee McCurdy Nichols, *The Royal Line of McCurdy* (Pittsburgh: Rosedog Press, 2013), 3.

38. McCurdy Nichols, *The Royal Line of McCurdy*, 4.

39. Regan, *Sketches and Traditions of the Northwest Arm*, 16.

40. Regan, *Sketches & Traditions of the Northwest Arm*, 49.

41. George Patterson, *A History of the County of Pictou, Nova Scotia* (Montreal: Dawson Brothers, 1877), 458.

42. *Truro Daily News*, September 16, 1904, 7.

43. The Monymusk Estate, www.monymusk.com.

44. John Burke, *A Genealogical and Heraldic Dictionary of the Peerage and Baronetage of the British Empire* (London: Henry Colburn, 1845), 408.

45. *Sydney Daily Post*, August 31, 1901.

46. *Morning Chronicle*, April 8, 1862, 3.

47. *British Colonist*, June 5, 1855, 2.

48. William Chambers, *A History of Peeblesshire* (Edinburgh: William and Robert Chambers, 1864), 325.

49. William Chambers, *Memoir of Robert Chambers with Autobiographic Reminiscences of William Chambers*, 3rd. ed. (New York: Scribner, Armstrong, and Co, 1872), 30.

50. W. and R. Chambers, *Peebles and Its Neighbourhood With a Run on Peebles Railway* (Edinburgh: John Menzies and Robert Stirling, 1856), 42.

51. Chambers, *Memoir of Robert Chambers*, 38.

52. Author's interview with Bell descendant, Sara Grosvenor, July 20, 2015.

53. Charlotte I. Perkins, *Old Houses of Annapolis Royal N.S.* (Saint John, NB: Barnes & Co., 1925), 21.

54. James Buist, *National Record of the Visit of Queen Victoria to Scotland, 1842* (Perth: The Perth Printing Company, 1842), 243.

55. *Truro Daily News*, September 19, 1906, 5.

56. *Morning Herald*, November 12, 1880.

57. Map of the Town of Dartmouth, H. W. Hopkins, Provincial Surveying and Pub. Co., 1878, Nova Scotia Archives.

58. *Truro Daily News*, August 21, 1905, 7.

59. *Truro Daily News*, November 27, 1918, 4.

60. Davidson/Davison Family File, Colchester Historical Society, accessed May 2016.

61. *Truro Daily News*, June 23, 1898, 2.

62. John Lovell, *Lovell's Canadian Dominion Directory for 1871* (Montreal: J. Lovell, 1871), 1622.

63. Regan, *Sketches and Traditions of the Northwest Arm*, 144.

64. A Lady, the Wife of a Naval Officer, *An Account of the Celebration of the Jubilee* (Birmingham: self-published, 1810), 7.

65. *McAlpine's Halifax City Directory 1878–79*, 158.

66. *The Braille Review*, January 1915, 254.

67. Janet Guildford, "Fraser, Sir Charles Frederick," in *Dictionary of Canadian Biography*, vol. 15, University of

Toronto/Université Laval, 2003–, accessed April 6, 2016, http://www.biographi.ca/en/bio/fraser_charles_frederick_15E.html.

68. *Truro Daily News*, November 30, 1918, 6.

69. *Truro Daily News*, August 30, 1915, 2.

70. *Truro Daily News*, July 13, 1915, 5.

71. *Truro Daily News*, July 8, 1915, 7.

72. *Truro Daily News*, July 13, 1915, 5.

73. *Truro Daily News*, January 8, 1906, 4.

74. Acadia University, *Memorials of Acadia College and Horton Academy for the Half-century 1828–1878* (Montreal: Dawson Brothers, 1881), 199.

CHAPTER 3

75. Aruthur W. Wallace, *An Album of Drawings of Early Buildings in Nova Scotia* (Halifax: Heritage Trust of Nova Scotia and the Nova Scotia Museum Halifax, 1976).

76. *Truro Daily News*, December 28, 1896.

77. *Truro Daily News*, October 19, 1907, 1.

78. Charles A. Armour, "Lawrence, William Dawson," in *Dictionary of Canadian Biography*, vol. 11, University of Toronto/Université Laval, 2003–, accessed November 22, 2013, http://www.biographi.ca/en/bio/lawrence_william_dawson_11E.html.

79. "King Athelstan (924–939)," Britroyals, http://www.britroyals.com/kings.asp?id=athelstan, n.d.

80. Rev. Samuel Lodge, *Scrivelsby, The Home of the Champions* (Horncastle: W. K. Morton, 1893), ix.

81. Lodge, *Scrivelsby, The Home of the Champions*, 22–23.

82. Joseph Dimock Marsters, *A Genealogy of the Dimock Family from the Year 1637* (Windsor, NS: n.p., 1899), 8.

83. J. D. Marsters, *A Genealogy of the Dimock Family from the Year 1637*, 22.

84. D. A. Sutherland, "Johnston, James William," in *Dictionary of Canadian Biography*, vol. 10, University of Toronto/Université Laval, 2003–, accessed November 12, 2013, http://www.biographi.ca/en/bio/johnston_james_william_10E.html.

85. Sutherland, "Johnston, James William."

86. K. G. Pryke, "Johnston, James William (1792–1873)," *Oxford Dictionary of National Biography* (Oxford: Oxford University Press, 2004), accessed November 12, 2013, http://www.oxforddnb.com/view/article/54618.

87. *British Colonist*, August 29, 1850, 2.

88. *British Colonist*, March 12, 1874, 2.

89. Mrs. William Lawson, *History of The Townships of Dartmouth, Preston and Lawrencetown* edited by Harry Piers (Halifax: Morton and Co., 1893), 101.

90. *Truro Daily News*, September 26, 1914, 5.

91. Nicholas Lusher, *Biography of William T. James* (New York: The Lusher Gallery LLC, n.d.

92. Judith Fingard, "Inglis, Charles," in *Dictionary of Canadian Biography*, vol. 5, University of Toronto/Université Laval, 2003–, accessed April 6, 2015, http://www.biographi.ca/en/bio/inglis_charles_5E.html.

93. A. W. H. Eaton, *The History of King's County, Nova Scotia, Heart of the Acadian Land* (Salem, MA: Salem Press Company, 1910), 701.

94. *Truro Daily News*, August 18, 1917, 3.

95. D. W. Johnson, *History of Methodism in Eastern British America* (Sackville, NB: Tribune Printing, 1926), 35.

96. Johnson, *History of Methodism in Eastern British America*, 95.

97. Johnson, *History of Methodism in Eastern British America*, 35 and 370.

98. Johnson, *History of Methodism in Eastern British America*, 381.

99. Suzanne Zeller, "Lawson, George," in *Dictionary of Canadian Biography*, vol. 12, University of Toronto/Université Laval, 2003–, accessed March 3, 2016, http://www.biographi.ca/en/bio/lawson_george_12E.html.

100. Mary R. S. Creese, *Ladies in the Laboratory III* (Lanham, MD: Scarecrow Press, 2010), 146–147.

101. *The Proceedings and Transactions of the Nova Scotia Institute of Science 1890–94*, vol. 8 (1895): 91.

102. *Chronicle Herald*, February 26, 2007.

103. Marion Christie, "Growing Up in Bedford 1914–1930," A presentation given at Scott Manor House later adapted to an online presentation, slides #187 and #189 (accessed May 1, 2017) http://www.virtualmuseum.ca/sgc-cms/histoires_de_chez_nous-community_memories/pm_v2.php?id=story_line&lg=English&fl=0&ex=00000518&sl=3990&pos=1&pf=1#159.

104. *British Colonist*, July 7, 1857, 3.

105. B. C. Cuthbertson, "Uniacke, Richard John (1753–1830)," in Dictionary of Canadian Biography, vol. 7, University of Toronto/Université Laval, 2003–, accessed May 1, 2017, http://www.biographi.ca/en/bio/uniacke_richard_john_1753_1830_6E.html.

106. *McAlpine's Halifax City Directory 1878–79* (Halifax: David McAlpine, Nova Scotia Printing Company, 1878), 275.

107. *McAlpine's Halifax City Directory 1889–90*, 261.

108. *The Daily Sun* May 2, 1892.

109. *Truro Daily News*, September 7, 1909, 5.

CHAPTER 4

110. Regan, *Sketches and Traditions of the Northwest Arm*, 146.

111. *Halifax Herald*, May 21, 1904, 11.

112. *Truro Daily News*, October 9, 1908, 5.

113. A. F. Church map of Antigonish, c. 1877, Antigonish Heritage Museum.

114. *Truro Daily News*, May 28, 1907, 8.

115. *Truro Daily News*, April 4, 1898, 1.

116. *Truro Daily News*, June 4, 1892, 1.

117. *Yarmouth Herald*, March 6, 1873, 3.

118. *Yarmouth Herald*, October 6, 1870, 4.

119. *Halifax Herald*, June 30, 1904, 2.

120. *Truro Daily News*, July 28, 1894, 1.

121. Thomas Nuttall, *The Genera of North American Plants and a Catalogue of the Species, to the Year 1817* (Philadelphia: D. Heartt, 1818), 115.

122. *Truro Daily News*, May 22, 1907, 5.

123. *Truro Daily News*, August 29, 1917, 5.

124. *Truro Daily News*, October 22, 1917, 4.

125. *Truro Daily News*, September 26, 1917, 4.

126. *Truro Daily News*, May 8, 1918, 5.

127. Loran DeWolfe, *Nature Study Hints* (Truro: n.p., 1919), 107.

128. *Truro Daily News*, September 13, 1918, 5.

129. Regan, *Sketches and Traditions of the Northwest Arm*, 31.

130. Regan, *Sketches and Traditions of the Northwest Arm*, 21.

131. "The Birchdale on the Shores of the Northwest Arm," (brochure), c. 1908.

132. "The Birchdale on the Shores of the Northwest Arm."

133. Regan, *Sketches and Traditions of the Northwest Arm*, 36.

134. *Digby Weekly Courier*, July 21, 1905, 2.

135. *Truro Daily News*, February 10, 1919, 3.

136. *Truro Daily News*, August 24, 1893, 1.

137. Almon C. Varney, *Our Homes and Their Adornments* (Detroit: J. C. Chilton, 1882), 321.

138. Ella Rodman Church, *How to Furnish a Home* (New York: D. Appleton and Co., 1882), 122.

139. *Halifax Herald,* June 18, 1908, 10.

140. *Truro Daily News*, August 21, 1907, 7.

141. Regan, *Sketches and Traditions of the Northwest Arm*, 57.

142. *Truro Daily News*, May 20, 1908, 5.

143. *Halifax Herald,* July 10, 1909, 5.

144. *Halifax Herald,* July 9, 1908, 4.

145. *Daily News* (Saint John), October 10, 1877.

146. *Truro Daily News*, October 9, 1899, 2.

147. *Truro Daily News,* July 9, 1910, 8.

148. *Yarmouth Herald*, April 3, 1873, 3.

149. *Truro Daily News*, November 2, 1915, 5.

150. Natalie Clerk, *Prescott House, Starrs Point, Nova Scotia*, (Ottawa: Environment Canada–Parks, 1987), 5.

151. Clerk, *Prescott House, Starrs Point, Nova Scotia*, 4.

152. William Prescott, *The Prescott Memorial: or a Genealogical Memoir of the Prescott Families in America* (Boston: Henry W. Dutton & Son, 1870), 86.

153. William Cobbett, *The Woodlands* (London: William Cobbett, 1825),329.

154. Donald Culross Peattie, *A Natural History of North American Trees* (San Antonia: Trinity University Press, 2007), 338–339.

155. *Scientific American*, July 12, 1890, 25.

156. Cobbett, *The Woodlands*, 351.

157. *Scientific American*, July 12, 1890, 25.

158. Cobbett, *The Woodlands*, 326.

159. Cobbett, *The Woodlands*, 328.

160. Culross Peattie, *A Natural History of North American Trees*, 339.

161. A. L. Howard, *Trees in Britain* (London: Collins, 1946).

162. A. J. Downing, *A Treatise on the Theory and Practice of Landscape Gardening* (New York: Wiley and Putnam, 1841), 145.

163. John Brown Cuno, "Utilization of Black Locust" (Washington, DC: US Department of Agriculture, 1930), 15.

164. Brown Cuno, "Utilization of Black Locust," 15.

165. *Presbyterian Witness*, September 6, 1879, 284.

166. L. A. DeWolfe, *Nature Study Hints* (Truro: n.p., 1919), 131–132.

167. *Truro Daily News*, August 13, 1918, 4.

CHAPTER 5

168. *Halifax Herald,* July 6, 1909, 6.

169. *Acadian Recorder*, October 31, 1857, 1.

170. *Truro Daily News*, December 22, 1910, 4.

171. Charles Dickens, *Bleak House* (London: Bradbury & Evans, 1853), 68.

172. *British Colonist*, February 23, 1854, 2.

173. *British Colonist*, February 14, 1854, 3.

174. *Truro Daily News*, July 18, 1916, 5.

175. *Truro Daily News*, December 1, 1910, 8.

176. *Truro Daily News,* January 17, 1914, 5.

177. *Truro Daily News*, September 1, 1914, 5.

178. *Truro Daily News*, August 2, 1915, 5.

179. *Truro Daily News*, July 29, 1916, 5.

180. L.M. Montgomery, *Emily of New Moon* (Toronto: McClelland and Stewart, 1923), 97.

181. *Halifax Herald*, May 28, 1908, 2.

182. Philip Girard, "Weatherbe, Sir Robert Linton," in *Dictionary of Canadian Biography*, vol. 14, University of

Toronto/Université Laval, 2003–, accessed January 20, 2015, http://www.biographi.ca/en/bio/weatherbe_robert_linton_14E.html.

183. Waverley Heritage Museum, "History of Waverley," waverleycommunity.ca/wp-content/uploads/2010/09/History-of-Waverley.pdf.

184. Lawson, *History of the Townships of Dartmouth, Preston and Lawrencetown*, 104.

185. Thomas J. Brown, *Place-Names of the Province of Nova Scotia* (Halifax: NS Royal Print. & Litho., 1922), 151.

186. *British Colonist*, September 1, 1855, 3.

187. *Truro Daily News*, November 8, 1898, 3.

188. *Morning Chronicle*, October 18, 1873, 3.

189. A. F. Church map of Antigonish, c. 1877, Antigonish Heritage Museum.

190. *Truro Daily News*, November 11, 1918, 7.

191. *McAlpine's Halifax City Directory 1895–96*, 364.

192. *Truro Daily News*, October 19, 1891, 3.

193. William J. Anderson, *The Life of Edward, Duke of Kent* (Ottawa: Hunter, Rose, 1870), 42.

194. Judith Fingard, "Wentworth, Sir John," in *Dictionary of Canadian Biography*, vol. 5, University of Toronto/Université Laval, 2003–, accessed May 12, 2015, http://www.biographi.ca/en/bio/wentworth_john_1737_1820_5E.html.

195. *Seasoned Timbers*, Heritage Trust of Nova Scotia, 1962 p24

196. Frank M. Tierney, ed., *The Thomas Chandler Haliburton Symposium*, University of Ottawa Press, 1985 13.

197. *Halifax Herald*, July 19, 1904, 9.

198. Benson John Lossing, *The Hudson, From the Wilderness to the Sea* (New York: Virtue and Yorston, 1866).

199. *British Colonist*, May 3, 1855, 3 and June 9, 1855, 3.

200. William C. Bryant, *A Discourse on the Life, Character and Genius of Washington Irving* (New York: G. P. Putnam, 1860), 99.

201. Downing, *A Treatise on the Theory and Practice of Landscape Gardening*, 38.

202. *British Colonist*, April 24, 1855, 3.

203. *Truro Daily News*, May 25, 1897, 2.

204. *Truro Daily News*, May 5, 1916, 1.

205. *Truro Daily News*, April 9, 1910, 7.

206. *Digby Weekly Courier*, September 18, 1903, 4.

207. *Digby Weekly Courier*, August 18, 1905, 2.

208. *Halifax Herald*, July 22, 1909, 2.

209. *Truro Daily News*, March 5, 1918, 5.

210. *Truro Daily News*, July 29, 1897, 1.

211. *Truro Daily News*, April 2, 1907, 7.

212. Regan, *Sketches and Traditions of the Northwest Arm*, 90–91.

213. John Hughes, ed., *The Boscobel Tracts*, 2nd ed. (Edinburgh: W. Blackwood and Sons, 1857), 376.

214. Regan, *Sketches and Traditions of the Northwest Arm*, 139.

215. Terry Punch, "The Estates and Haunts of Dutch Village," *NSHQ* (1975 special supplement): 9.

216. Rev. J. R. Campbell, *A History of the County of Yarmouth, Nova Scotia* (Saint John: J. & A. McMillan, 1876), 40.

217. Brown, *Place-Names of the Province of Nova Scotia*, 65.

218. Campbell, *A History of the County of Yarmouth, Nova Scotia*, 40.

219. *Morning Chronicle*, August 12, 1873, 3.

220. *Royal Gazette and the Nova-Scotia Advertiser*, June 8, 1790, 1.

221. Regan, *Sketches and Traditions of the Northwest Arm*, 149.

222. Minerva Tracy, "De Mille, James," in *Dictionary of Canadian Biography*, vol. 10,

University of Toronto/Université Laval, 2003–, accessed January 29, 2015, http://www.biographi.ca/en/bio/de_mille_james_10E.html.

CHAPTER 6

223. *Truro Daily News*, July 5, 1906, 4.

224. *Truro Daily News*, July 5, 1906, 4.

225. *Truro Daily News*, October 30, 1906, 6.

226. *Colchester Sun*, October 1, 1890, 4.

227. *Colchester Sun*, October 1, 1890, 4.

228. *Colchester Sun*, October 1, 1890, 4.

229. William A. Calnek, *History of the County of Annapolis*, edited by Alfred Savary (Toronto: William Briggs, 1897), 289–290.

230. Heritage Trust of Nova Scotia, *Founded Upon a Rock: Historic Buildings of Halifax and Vicinity* (Halifax: Heritage Trust of Nova Scotia, 1967), 108.

231. Lawson, *History of the Townships of Dartmouth, Preston and Lawrencetown*, 179.

232. *N.S. Royal Gazette*, September 10, 1801.

233. Lawson, *History of the Townships of Dartmouth, Preston and Lawrencetown*, 178.

234. Lawson, *History of the Townships of Dartmouth, Preston and Lawrencetown*, 183.

235. Department of Northern Affairs and Natural Resources, *The Halifax Citadel* (Queen's Printer and Controller of Stationery, 1954), 7.

236. Raymond A. MacLean, ed., *History of Antigonish*, vol. 2 (Halifax: Formac, 1976), 105.

237. Ronald H. Mcdonald, "Tonge, Winckworth," in *Dictionary of Canadian Biography*, vol. 4, University of Toronto/Université Laval, 2003–, accessed April 27, 2016, http://www.biographi.ca/en/bio/tonge_winckworth_4E.html.

238. John Wilson, "The Story of Winckworth Tonge," West Hants Historical Society newsletter January, 2013.

239. *Royal Gazette and the Nova-Scotia Advertiser*, April 1, 1800, 3.

240. *Presbyterian Witness*, April 25, 1868, 136.

241. *McAlpine's Directory of Halifax 1878–79*, 187.

242. *Halifax and Provincial Real Estate Register: January 1878* (Halifax: J. Naylor, 1878), 7.

243. *Truro Daily News*, February 19, 1897, 3.

244. Jacqueline Banerjee, "Dear Old Claremont": Queen Victoria and Surrey's Royal Estate, Victorian Web, 2013, http://www.victorianweb.org/art/architecture/claremont/1.html.

245. Perkins, *Old Houses of Annapolis Royal*, 14.

246. Isaiah W. Wilson, *A Geography and History of the County of Digby, Nova Scotia* (Halifax: Holloway Brothers, 1900), 5.

247. *Digby Weekly Courier*, June 16, 1905, 3.

248. John Dvorak, *The Last Volcano* (New York: Pegasus Books, 2015).

249. *St John Daily Sun*, August 5, 1904, 1.

250. *British Colonist*, October 20, 1857, 3.

CHAPTER 7

251. *Truro Daily News*, October 19, 1906, 1.

252. *Halifax Evening Reporter*, November 16, 1878.

253. *Colchester Sun*, January 2, 1878, 2.

254. *Truro Daily News*, September 14, 1898, 2.

255. Author unknown, "The Late Dr. Ambrose," *Church Work* vol. 23, no. 9 (November 1898): 131.

256. *Truro Daily News*, September 6, 1907, 8.

257. *Truro Daily News*, September 30, 1898, 1.

258. *Truro Daily News*, February 20, 1919, 4.

259. Alexander Reford, "Smith, Donald Alexander, 1st Baron Strathcona and Mount Royal," in vol. 14, University of Toronto/Université Laval, 2003–, accessed November 19, 2013, http://www.biographi.ca/en/bio/smith_donald_alexander_14E.html.

260. *Truro Daily News*, November, 2, 1896. 3.

261. *Truro Daily News*, March 16, 1897, 4.

262. *Truro Daily News*, May 9, 1903, 7.

263. William C. Archibald, *Home-Making and its Philosophy* (Boston: W. C. Archibald, 1910), 404.

264. *Truro Daily News*, October 16, 1899, 1.

265. Olga Neal, "The Saga of 'Rudder' Churchill," www.yarmouth.org/villages/darling/.

266. *Truro Daily News*, October 25, 1899, 6.

267. *Truro Daily News*, July 27, 1898, 3.

268. *Truro Daily News*, July 11, 1898, 4.

269. *Acadian Recorder*, May 7, 1864, 1.

270. Allan C. Dunlop, "Ritchie, Thomas," in *Dictionary of Canadian Biography*, vol. 8, University of Toronto/Université Laval, 2003–, accessed June 19, 2015, http://www.biographi.ca/en/bio/ritchie_thomas_8E.html.

271. Charlotte Isabella Perkins, *The Romance of Old Annapolis Royal Nova Scotia* (Historical Association of Annapolis Royal, 1952), 57.

272. *McAlpine's Halifax City Directory 1895–96*, 392.

273. Dr. David Rowe and Wendy Jacobs, *Former St. James's Presbyterian Church Heritage Assessment* Prepared for the City of Ballarat, 2012.

274. *British Colonist*, March 31, 1859, 1.

275. *Daily News* (Saint John), October 3, 1878.

276. *Timaru Herald*, August 13, 1878, 5.

277. *British Colonist*, April 28, 1860, 1.

278. *British Colonist*, November 1, 1855, 2.

279. William McCulloch, *The Life of Thomas McCulloch, D.D.* (n.p., 1920), 18–50.

CHAPTER 8

280. *Truro Daily News*, September 11, 1907, 2.

281. *Truro Daily News*, August 8, 1899, 8.

282. *Truro Daily News*, February 2, 1915, 5.

283. *Truro Daily News*, July 27, 1917, 7.

284. Lordly House Museum, "The American Connection," Slide 120 of 138, virtualmuseum.ca.

285. *Digby Weekly Courier*, September 9, 1904, 3.

286. *Morning Herald*, February 2, 1881.

287. *Truro Daily News*, October 13, 1904, 5.

288. *The Novascotian*, September 5, 1859.

289. *Daily Record*, September 14, 1900, 1.

290. A. F. Church Map of Antigonish County, c.1877, Antigonish Heritage Museum.

291. *Truro Daily News*, August 10, 1899, 2.

292. *Truro Daily News*, August 29, 1898, 1.

293. "Every One for Truro," September 14, 1897, "Truro Jubilee and Natal Celebration," 1897.

294. *Truro Daily News*, November 1, 1897, 3.

295. Map of the Town of Dartmouth, H. W. Hopkins, Provincial Surveying and Pub. Co., 1878, Nova Scotia Archives.

296. Regan, *Sketches and Traditions of the Northwest Arm*, 141.

297. *McAlpine's Halifax City Directory 1872–73*, 348.

298. Janet Chute, "Marlborough Woods Woodland Park," *Southender* (February 1999).

299. *Truro Daily News*, June 26, 1909, 1.

300. Chute, "Marlborough Woods Woodland Park."

301. *British Colonist*, May 19, 1857, 3.

302. *British Colonist*, May 19, 1857, 3.

303. *Morning Chronicle*, July 12, 1873, 2.

CHAPTER 9

304. Lawson, *History of The Townships of Dartmouth, Preston and Lawrencetown*, 110.

305. A. W .H. Eaton, *The History of King's County, Nova Scotia, Heart of the Acadian Land*, (Salem Press, 1910), 148.

306. H. B. Jefferson, "Mount Rundell, Stellarton, and the Albion Railway of 1839," *NSHS*, vol. 34 (1963): 87.

307. Jefferson, "Mount Rundell, Stellarton, and the Albion Railway of 1839," 90.

308. Jefferson, *Mount Rundell, Stellarton, and the Albion Railway of 1839*, 91.

309. Jefferson, *Mount Rundell, Stellarton, and the Albion Railway of 1839*, 94.

310. George Stewart Jr., *Canada Under the Administration of the Earl of Dufferin* (Toronto: Rose-Belford, 1878), 255–256.

311. Harriot Georgina Blackwood, Marchioness of Dufferin and Ava, *My Canadian Journal 1872–78*, (London: John Murray, 1891), 103.

312. *The Daily Telegraph*, April 16, 1888.

313. John Douglas Sutherland Campbell, *The Life of Queen Victoria* (London, 1909), 364.

314. Susan Buggey, "Downs, Andrew," in *Dictionary of Canadian Biography*, vol. 12, University of Toronto/Université Laval, 2003–, accessed January 2, 2014, http://www.biographi.ca/en/bio/downs_andrew_12E.html.

315. Campbell Hardy, "Sketches in Our Neighbourhood—An Afternoon with Downs," *Acadian Recorder*, 1864.

316. Charles Waterton, *Essays on Natural History, Chiefly Ornithology: With an Autobiography of the Author, and a View of Walton Hall* (London: Longman, Orme, Brown, Green, & Longmans, 1838).

317. Campbell Hardy, "Reminiscences of a Nova Scotian Naturalist: Andrew Downs," Nova Scotia Institute of Science, *Proc. and Trans.* 12 (1906).

318. Philip Girard, "Townshend, Sir Charles James," in *Dictionary of Canadian Biography*, vol. 15, University of Toronto/Université Laval, 2003–, accessed May 26, 2015, http://www.biographi.ca/en/bio/townshend_charles_james_15E.html.

319. *Halifax Herald*, May 28, 1908, 2.

CHAPTER 10

320. *Truro Daily News*, November 1, 1899.

321. *Truro Daily News*, November 7, 1918, 3.

322. *Truro Daily News*, July 19, 1900, 5.

323. *Halifax Herald*, July 12, 1909, 3.

324. Regan, *Sketches and Traditions of the Northwest Arm*, 122.

325. George Dodd, *The History of the Indian Revolt and the Expeditions to Persia, China, and Japan 1856-7-8* (London: W. and R. Chambers, 1859), 278.

326. Thomas B Akins, *History of Halifax City* (Halifax: [Nova Scotia Historical Society], 1895), 211.

327. *British Colonist*, June 15, 1857, 3.

328. "Report on Forts," 1816, PANS, RE53.

329. Charles M. Andrews, *Guide to the Materials for American History, to 1873*, vol. 2 (Washington, DC: Carnegie Institution of Washington, 1914), 83.

330. *British Colonist*, May 22, 1858, 3.

331. C. C. Morton Bookseller and Stationer, *Morton's Guide to Halifax* (Halifax, 1878), 60.

332. Joseph Howe et al., *Collections of the Nova Scotia Historical Society*, vol. 17 (Halifax: Nova Scotia Historical Society, 1913), 42.

333. *Morning Journal*, October 27, 1854, 2.

334. C. H. Belcher, *Belcher's Farmer's Almanack* (Halifax: C. H. Belcher, 1856), 100.

335. Tony Edwards, *Historic Bedford* (Halifax: Nimbus Publishing, 2007), 150.

CHAPTER 11

336. *Truro Daily News*, July 31, 1905, 7.

337. *Truro Daily News*, July 31, 1905, 7.

338. *Digby Weekly Courier*, September 9, 1904, 3.

339. *British Colonist*, April 25, 1850, 3.

340. J. H. Meacham and Company, *Illustrated Historical Atlas of Pictou County, Nova Scotia* (Pictou: J. H. Meacham and Company, 1879), 12.

341. *Truro Daily News*, January 15, 1901, 8.

342. *Truro Daily News*, September 24, 1918, 5.

343. *Truro Daily News*, January 22, 1916, 2.

344. Rev. Silas T. Rand, *Dictionary of the Language of the Micmac Indians* (Halifax: Nova Scotia Printing Co., 1888), 217–218.

345. Judith Fingard, "Rand, Silas Tertius," in *Dictionary of Canadian Biography*, vol. 11, University of Toronto/Université Laval, 2003–, accessed March 10, 2015, http://www.biographi.ca/en/bio/rand_silas_tertius_11E.html.

346. *Digby Weekly Courier*, July 13, 1877, 4.

347. *Truro Daily News*, July 15, 1895, 3.

348. *Halifax Herald*, July 16, 1909, 6.

349. *Presbyterian Witness*, November 16, 1878, 365.

350. *British Colonist*, August 4, 1860, 2.

351. Advertisement flier, Nova Scotia Archives, MG100 vol. 29, no. 63, 1857.

352. *British Colonist*, November 6, 1851, 3.

353. Lawson, *History of the Townships of Dartmouth, Preston and Lawrencetown*, 136–137.

354. Regan, *Sketches and Traditions of the Northwest Arm*, 94.

355. *The Outlook*, June 15, 1896, 1066.

356. *Daily Sun* (Saint John), August 12, 1885.

357. *Morning Chronicle*, July 11, 1873, 1.

358. *American Agriculturalist*, vol. 34 (1875): 117.

359. *Truro Daily News*, July 5, 1892, 4.

360. *Truro Daily News*, July 24, 1903, 8.

361. *Truro Daily News*, April 6, 1916, 8.

362. *Truro Daily News*, September 21, 1915, 1.

363. *Truro Daily News*, November 10, 1915, 8.

364. *Presbyterian Witness*, June 17, 1865, 192.

365. *Truro Daily News*, April 20, 1910, 6.

366. *Digby Weekly Courier*, March 16, 1900, 2.

367. *Truro Daily News*, May 3, 1910, 6.

368. *Digby Weekly Courier*, March 16, 1900, 2.

369. *Digby Weekly Courier*, April 3, 1903, 4.

370. Chute, "Marlborough Woods Woodland Park."

CONCLUSION

371. *Truro Daily News*, May 22, 1907, 5.

372. The *Truro Daily News* issues researched span the years 1891–1920.

IMAGE
SOURCES